2400

FEDERAL ENERGY INFORMATION SOURCES
AND DATA BASES

FEDERAL ENERGY INFORMATION SOURCES AND DATA BASES

Carolyn C. Bloch

NOYES DATA CORPORATION

Park Ridge, New Jersey, U.S.A.

1979

Copyright © 1979 by Carolyn C. Bloch
No part of this book may be reproduced in any form
without permission in writing from the Publisher.
Library of Congress Catalog Card Number: 79-15543
ISBN: 0-8155-0764-X
Printed in the United States

Published in the United States of America by
Noyes Data Corporation
Noyes Building, Park Ridge, New Jersey 07656

Library of Congress Cataloging in Publication Data
Bloch, Carolyn.
  Federal energy information sources and data
bases.

  Includes index.
  1. Energy policy--Information services--United
States. 2. Administrative agencies--Information
services--United States. 3. United States--
Executive departments. 4. Power resources--United
States. I. Title.
HD9502.U52B58   016.3337   79-15543
ISBN 0-8155-0764-X

Foreword

This directory comprises all federal government agencies, departments, offices and cooperating information sources that deal in some capacity with energy—civilian, military and legislative.

Determining the proper agency as a source of energy information can be as perplexing as making use of the information once it is obtained. Federal agencies amass myriad amounts of data and store it away. Successful retrieval of this information can serve as an economical bibliographic tool for scientists, managers and engineers.

This time-saving directory of information sources and data bases supplies the address and a capsule description of each source, delineating its field of emphasis, services offered and, many times, availability of publications aside from the departmental reports which are usually provided free of charge.

A most valuable asset of this book is the four interrelated indexes: General; Information Centers; Information Retrieval Systems; and the index of Libraries. The reader should also make use of the clear, expanded table of contents which precedes the text.

Contents

INTRODUCTION 1

SECTION I. CABINET DEPARTMENTS

DEPARTMENT OF ENERGY. 4
Libraries 4
Department of Energy Library, Washington, DC 4
Research Centers Libraries 5
DOE Government-Owned/Contractor-Operated Laboratory and Facility
Libraries 6
Department of Energy Centers and Systems 12
Argonne National Laboratory 12
Bonneville Power Administration 13
Brookhaven National Laboratory 14
Lawrence Berkeley Laboratory 15
Lawrence Livermore Laboratory 16
LMFBR Fuel Cladding Information Center. 17
Nevada Operations Office 17
Oak Ridge Tennessee Information Centers 18
Regional Energy/Environment Information Centers. 27
Other DOE Information Centers and Systems. 29
Energy Information Administration 31
National Energy Information Center. 31
Office of Energy Data of Interpretation. .31

DEPARTMENT OF AGRICULTURE 33
National Agricultural Library. 33
Agricola. 33

DEPARTMENT OF COMMERCE. 34
National Technical Information Service (NTIS). 34

NTIS Bibliographic Data File. 34
Energy Publications. 35
Government-Owned Patent Data 38
Foreign Technology and Translations 38
Order Information for NTIS Publications. .40
Patent Office 41
Patent Search Files 41
Scientific Library at the Patent and Trademark Office 41
Office of Technology Assessment and Forecast. 42
District Offices. 43
National Bureau of Standards 43
Library 43
National Standard Reference Data System (NSRDS) 44
Data Analysis Centers. 44
Center for Building Technology Information 50
National Oceanic Atmospheric Administration 50

DEPARTMENT OF DEFENSE 52
Library and Analysis Centers. 52
Defense Nuclear Agency Technical Library Division. 52
Defense Analysis Centers 52
Navy. 54
Laboratories. 54
Army 55
Army Research Office 55
Redstone Scientific Information Center. 56
Harry Diamond Labs, Science and Technical Information Office 56
Army Mobility Equipment Research and Development Command,
    Ft Belvoir Technical Library 56
Army Materiel Development & Readiness Command, Science and
    Technology Division 56
Air Force. 57
Aero Propulsion Lab, Wright Patterson AFB, Ohio. 57
Air Force Geophysics Lab, Hanscom AFB Technical Library 57
Air Force Weapons Lab, Kirtland AFB Technical Library 57
Office of Science Research, Bolling Field AFB Technical Library 58
Office of Scientific Research, Bolling Field AFB, Documents Section . .58
Tri Service Industry Information Center 58
Navy Acquisition Research and Development Center 58
Army Research, Development and Planning Information for Industry . .59
Air Force Information for Industry Office 59
Defense Documentation Center 60
Data Banks. 60
Other Services Offered 61
Announcements of DDC Programs, Products and Services. 62
Eligibility Requirements. 62
Registration 62
Ordering Publications. 62
Classified Information 62
How DDC Serves the General Public 63
Service to Legal Profession 63
Unclassified/Unlimited DOD Reports 63
Service Continued Between Contracts 64

How to Find Information on the Potential Defense Contractors
   Program. 64

DEPARTMENT OF HOUSING AND URBAN DEVELOPMENT 65
   Information Sources and Systems. 65
      National Solar Heating and Cooling Information Center 65
      National Solar Heating and Cooling Solar Documentation Center 65

DEPARTMENT OF INTERIOR. 66
   U.S. Geological Survey. 66
      Energy Resources Data Systems. 66
      Crib Mineral Resources. 67
      Information Analysis Centers and Systems. 67

DEPARTMENT OF TRANSPORTATION 70
   Library 70
   Information Systems, Trisnet. 70
      Core Services 71

SECTION II. ADMINISTRATIVE AGENCIES

ENVIRONMENTAL PROTECTION AGENCY. 74
   Library 74
   Information Sources and Systems. 74
      Office of Air Quality Planning and Standards 74
      Environmental Monitoring and Support Laboratory. 75
      Air Pollution Technical Information Center 75
      Solid Waste Information Retrieval System 75

GENERAL SERVICES ADMINISTRATION 77
   Data Bank on U.S. Resources. 77

NASA. 78
   Library 78
      Library Network (NALNET). 78
   Informational Sources and Systems. 78
      Research and Technology Objectives and Plans Summary 78
      NASA Scientific and Technical Information System. 79
      NASA/SCAN 79
      RECON. 79
      AIAA Technology Information Service 80
      Periodic Bibliographies. 80
      Office of Technology Utilization 80
      Industrial Application Centers 81
      National Space Science Data Center 82
      COSMIC 82
      NASA Patent Information. 82

NATIONAL SCIENCE FOUNDATION. 84
   Applied Science and Research Applications 84
   Directorate for Scientific Technological and International Affairs. 85
      Division of Policy Research and Analysis. 85
      Science Resources Studies. 85

NUCLEAR REGULATORY COMMISSION 87
    Nuclear Regulatory Commission Library 87

SECTION III. QUASI-GOVERNMENT AGENCIES

SMITHSONIAN SCIENCE INFORMATION EXCHANGE 90
    Search Services Available 90
    SSIE On-Line Search Service 91

SECTION IV. CONGRESSIONAL OFFICES

CONGRESSIONAL BUDGET OFFICE 94
    Information Sources and Systems. 94
        Congressional Scorekeeping System 94

GENERAL ACCOUNTING OFFICE. 95
    Information Sources and Systems. 95
        Legislative Authorization Program Information System 95

GOVERNMENT PRINTING OFFICE. 96
    Publications 96
    Ordering Information. 97

LIBRARY OF CONGRESS. 98
    Information Sources 98
    Congressional Research Service 99

OFFICE OF TECHNOLOGY ASSESSMENT 100
    Information Sources 100
        Office of Information. 100

INDEXES 101
    General 101
    Information Centers. 109
    Information Retrieval Systems. 113
    Libraries 114

Introduction

The Federal agencies contain a valuable network of energy information. It is the intention of this directory to make it easier to identify, acquire, and compile this up-to-date Federal energy data that are constantly needed in the scientific and technical community. This information can prove to be an easy and economical reference tool especially for those scientists, managers, and engineers concerned with budgetary problems, proposal preparations and all the other forms of energy research studies and projects.

The scope of the directory covers all the agencies that deal in some capacity with energy problems. Included is a compilation of energy data sources not only from the civilian agencies, but also from the military sector and some of the legislative sources for information. Environmental and toxicology sources are also included along with the energy data. This was done because energy sources can cause particular environmental problems. In the future environmental problems may play an even bigger role in energy research. A compilation of all the aspects and sources of energy information helps to present a more complete picture of the available energy data.

The directory contains not only information on the sources, but also services offered and in many cases availability of publications. This data changes periodically within the Federal government. However, knowing the present sources of information will help individuals to locate new energy information as it appears within the public sector.

The information was compiled from a number of sources. One source was the directory *Federal Information Sources and Systems.* This publication is part of the Congressional Sourcebook Series available from GPO. The data are voluminous and it was necessary to analyze and determine the information that was pertinent to the energy field.

Another source that proved helpful was the *Defense Documentation Center Referral Data Bank Directory.* This consists of computer printouts that contain specialized information on resources that serve the scientific community. Another publication that presented important energy sources was the *Directory of Libraries and Information Specialists in Department of Energy and Its Contractor Organizations.* Information was also received from the various Federal government publications and pamphlets.

Lastly, conversations with individuals involved in the Federal energy field proved to be extremely important in compiling a directory of this type.

Relevant work is continually being accomplished in the public sector, so that hopefully this publication will help the private sector obtain time-saving utilization of Federal energy materials for nominal costs.

SECTION I
CABINET DEPARTMENTS

Department of Energy

1000 Independence Ave., SW
Washington, DC 20545
Locator (202) 252-5000
Public Inquiry (202) 252-5568

LIBRARIES

DEPARTMENT OF ENERGY LIBRARY, WASHINGTON, DC

Description: Contains monograph collection of approximately 40,000 titles. The microfiche collection has close to one-half million documents and the journal collection contains approximately 2,300 titles. The library is a selected depository for the Government Printing Office, and provides on-line searching on DOE RECON, Lockheed, SDC, JURIS, MEDLINE, Dow Jones, NASA RECON, BRS, OCLC and the New York Times information systems. The automated systems provide access to the monograph journal, GPO reports, DOE publication collection and MARC.

Contact: Library
Department of Energy Library
20 Massachusetts Ave., NW
Washington, DC 20545

Library
Germantown
Mail Station G042
Washington, DC 20545

Library
Room 8501
825 North Capitol Street, NE
Washington, DC 20426

RESEARCH CENTERS LIBRARIES

Bartlesville Energy Research Center Library

Description: Emphasis is on petroleum and natural gas. On-line bibliographic searching, and reference services.

Contact: Bartlesville Energy Research Center Library
PO Box 1398
Bartlesville, OK 74003
Telephone (918) 336-2400

Grand Forks Energy Research Center Library

Description: Emphasis is on solid fuels, engineering, physical sciences, mathematics and environmental control.

Contact: Grand Forks Energy Research Center Library
Box 8213
University Station
Grand Forks, ND 58202
Telephone (701) 775-4207

Laramie Energy Research Center Library

Description: Emphasis is on chemistry, oil shale, petroleum, geology, coal, tar sands, engineering, and fossil fuel energy. On site public use of the collection and referral.

Contact: Laramie Energy Research Center Library
PO Box 3395
University Station
Laramie, WY 82071
Telephone (307) 721-2201

Morgantown Energy Research Center Library

Description: Emphasis is on chemistry, physics, coal, petroleum, fossil fuels, computers, infrared spectroscopy, mass spectroscopy, coal gasification, gas production, Devonian Shale and underground coal gasification.

Contact: Morgantown Energy Research Center Library
PO Box 880
Morgantown, WV 26505
Telephone (304) 599-7183

Pittsburgh Energy Research Center Library

Description: Emphasis is on nonnuclear information.

Contact: Pittsburgh Energy Research Center Library
4800 Forbes Ave.
Pittsburgh, PA 15213
Telephone (412) 892-2400

DOE GOVERNMENT-OWNED/CONTRACTOR-OPERATED LABORATORY AND FACILITY LIBRARIES

Ames Laboratory Library

Description: Information includes R&D reports published by the laboratory staff.

Contact: Ames Laboratory Library
Iowa State University
Ames, IA 50011
Telephone (515) 294-1856

Argonne National Laboratory Library

Description: Emphasis is on nuclear science, engineering, biological sciences, chemistry, energy, environmental sciences, materials science, mathematics and physics.

Contact: Argonne National Laboratory Library
Technical Information Services
Department Building 203
9700 South Cass Avenue
Argonne, IL 60439
Telephone (312) 972-4221

Battelle-Northwest Library and Information Services

Description: Emphasis is on nuclear science and engineering, metallurgy, materials, radiological sciences, environmental sciences, chemistry, physics and mathematics. Library serves the information needs of individuals at the Hanford Plant.

Contact: Battelle-Northwest Library and Information Services
Pacific Northwest Laboratory
PO Box 999
Richland, WA 99352
Telephone (509) 942-3443

Bendix Corporation—Technical Information Center

Description: Emphasis is on electrical and electronics, metals, plastics, engineering and chemistry. Comprehensive index and abstract services, including a DOE/RECON terminal provide bibliographic identification of all forms of information needed to serve the scientific, technical and managerial areas.

Contact: Bendix Corporation—Technical Information Center
Kansas City Division
PO Box 1159
Kansas City, MO 64141
Telephone (816) 997-2281

Bendix Field Engineering Corporation—Technical Library

Description: Emphasis is on geology, uranium mining, chemistry, physics, electronics, related scientific and technical information, plus business publications and law materials.

Contact: Bendix Field Engineering Corporation—Technical Library
Grand Junction Technical Library
PO Box 1569
Grand Junction, CO 81581
Telephone (303) 242-8621

Bettis Atomic Power Laboratory Library

Description: Emphasis is on nuclear energy, metallurgy, engineering, physics, mathematics, and chemistry.

Contact: Bettis Atomic Power Laboratory Library
Westinghouse Electric Corporation
PO Box 79
West Mifflin, PA 15122
Telephone (412) 462-5000

Brookhaven National Laboratory Library

Description: Emphasis is on biology, chemistry, electronics, energy, engineering, environmental sciences, instrumentation, materials sciences, mathematics, medicine and physics.

Contact: Brookhaven National Laboratory Library
Associated Universities Inc.
Upton, Long Island, NY 11973
Telephone (516) 345-2123

Environmental Measurements Laboratory Library

Description: Emphasis is on aerosols, chemistry, radiochemistry, data processing, electronics, instrumentation, and oceanography.

Contact: Environmental Measurements Laboratory Library
376 Hudson Street
New York, NY 10014
Telephone (212) 620-3606

General Atomic Company Library

Description: Emphasis is on nuclear literature and related scientific fields. Very complete collection of DOE R&D reports. Open to the public by appointment.

Contact: General Atomic Company Library
PO Box 81608
San Diego, CA 92138
Telephone (714) 455-3322

General Electric Company—Philadelphia Library

Description: Emphasis is on solar energy, thermal energy, wind power and nuclear power. Library has the ability to query via GE R&D center data bases in science, management and engineering.

Contact: General Electric Company—Philadelphia Library
Space/RESD Library
PO Box 8555
Philadelphia, PA 19101
Telephone (215) 962-4700

General Electric Company—St. Petersburg Library

Description: Emphasis is on chemistry, physics, electronics, engineering and management with particular interest given to high vacuum technology and materials science.

Contact: General Electric Company—St. Petersburg Library
PO Box 11508
St. Petersburg, FL 33733
Telephone (813) 544-2511

Goodyear Atomic Corporation Library

Description: Emphasis is on atomic and nuclear science, uranium chemistry, physics, engineering, industrial safety, metallurgy, mathematics, and all branches of engineering.

Contact: Goodyear Atomic Corporation Library
PO Box 628
Piketon, OH 45661
Telephone (614) 289-2331

Idaho National Engineering Laboratory Technical Library

Description: Emphasis is on nuclear science, and peripheral fields such as chemistry, chemical engineering, instrumentation, metallurgy, computer sciences. Collection includes all fields of energy production and alternate energy sources.

Contact: Idaho National Engineering Laboratory Technical Library
EG&G Idaho Inc.
PO Box 1625
Idaho Falls, ID 83401
Telephone (208) 526-1196

Inhalation Toxicology Research Institute Library

Description: Emphasis is on inhalation toxicology, physics, chemistry of aerosols, and the biological and physical considerations of dose to tissues.

Contact: Inhalation Toxicology Research Institute Library
Lovelace Biomedical and Environmental Research Institute
PO Box 5890
Albuquerque, NM 87115
Telephone (505) 264-2600

Knolls Atomic Power Laboratory Library

Description: Emphasis is on naval nuclear engineering. Contains classified and unclassified government agency science and technical reports.

Contact: Knolls Atomic Power Laboratory Library
PO Box 1072
Schenectady, NY 12301
Telephone (518) 393-6611

Lawrence Berkeley Laboratory Library

Description: Emphasis is on nuclear physics, nuclear chemistry, and information on the laboratory's energy and environmental research programs.

Contact: Lawrence Berkeley Laboratory Library
Library Building 50
Room 134
Berkeley, CA 94720
Telephone (415) 843-2740

Lawrence Livermore Laboratory Library

Description: Emphasis is on physics, chemistry, engineering, materials sciences, mathematics, geology, biomedical sciences and environmental sciences. Library houses two hard-wired terminals to government sponsored retrieval networks (DOE RECON and DDC RDT&E system).

Contact: Lawrence Livermore Laboratory Library
University of California
PO Box 808
Livermore, CA 94550
Telephone (415) 422-9310

Los Alamos Scientific Laboratory Library

Description: Emphasis is on physical and biomedical sciences, engineering and energy. Compiles lists of all unclassified laboratory publications. Portion of unclassified collection available to public.

Contact: Los Alamos Scientific Laboratory Library
University of California
PO Box 1663, MS-180
Los Alamos, NM 87545
Telephone (505) 667-4355

Mason & Hanger, Silas Mason Co., Inc.—Amarillo Library

Description: Emphasis is on chemical explosives, engineering, environmental, health and safety engineering.

Contact: Mason & Hanger, Silas Mason Co., Inc.—Amarillo Library
Pantex Plant
PO Box 30020
Amarillo, TX 79177
Telephone (806) 335-1581

Mound Facilities Library

Description: Emphasis is on physical sciences, mathematics and technology.

Contact: Mound Facilities Library
                Monsanto Corp.
                PO Box 32
                Miamisburg, OH 45342
                Telephone (513) 866-7444

Oak Ridge Associated Universities Library

Description: Emphasis is on nuclear medicine and occupational medicine re-
                lated to energy production technology.

Contact: Oak Ridge Associated Universities Library
                Medical and Health Sciences
                PO Box 117
                Oak Ridge, TN 37830
                Telephone (615) 483-8411

Oak Ridge National Laboratory Library

Description: Emphasis is on biology, chemistry, physics, nuclear technology,
                metallurgy, environmental sciences and energy. The library pro-
                vides SDI services and computerized retrieval services including
                RECON, Lockheed DIALOG, SDC ORBIT, and the NY Times
                Information Bank.

Contact: Oak Ridge National Laboratory Library
                PO Box X
                Oak Ridge, TN 37830
                Telephone (615) 483-8611

Princeton University, Plasma Physics Laboratory, Library

Description: Emphasis is on plasma physics, controlled fusion and nuclear
                reactors. Reports, technical journals, conference proceedings
                and microfiche are abstracted and cataloged.

Contact: Princeton University Plasma Physics Laboratory, Library
                James Forrestal Campus
                PO Box 451
                Princeton, NJ 08540
                Telephone (609) 452-3254

Reynolds Electrical and Engineering Co. Technical Library

Description: Emphasis is on industrial hygiene, radiological safety and occu-
                pational medicine. Maintains close liaison with the Department
                of Energy and EG&G Las Vegas Technical Library.

Contact: Reynolds Electrical and Engineering Co. Technical Library
                M/S 707
                PO Box 14400
                Las Vegas, NV 89114
                Telephone (702) 986-0796

Rockwell International Library

Description: Emphasis is on atomic energy, environmental matters, metallurgy, chemistry, physics, mathematics, and engineering.

Contact: Rockwell International Library
Atomic International Division
Rocky Flats Plant
PO Box 938
Golden, CO 80401

Sandia Laboratories Library, Albuquerque

Description: Emphasis is on nuclear weapons, peaceful uses of nuclear energy, materials, ordnance, physics, solid state physics, mathematics, energy sources, space power systems, and environmental engineering. The library has two terminals dedicated to the DOE RECON and DDC DRDT&E retrieval systems.

Contact: Sandia Laboratories Library, Albuquerque
Technical Library
PO Box 5800
Albuquerque, NM 87115
Telephone (505) 264-8765

Sandia Laboratories Library, Livermore

Description: Emphasis is on nuclear ordnance, materials, physics, mathematics, environmental engineering, energy conversion and utilization.

Contact: Sandia Laboratories Library, Livermore
Organization 8266
Livermore, CA 94550
Telephone (415) 455-2525

Savannah River Laboratory Library

Description: Emphasis is on nuclear energy and environmental related subjects. Searches are aided by RECON, SDC and Lockheed computerized information retrieval systems.

Contact: Savannah River Laboratory Library
E.I. DuPont de Nemours & Co., Inc.
Aiken, SC 29801
Telephone (803) 824-6331

Southwest Research Institute Library

Description: Emphasis is on chemistry, physics, electronics, mathematics and engineering. Library is open to the public.

Contact: Southwest Research Institute Library
Thomas Baker Slick Memorial Library
PO Drawer 28510
San Antonio, TX 78284
Telephone (512) 684-5111

Stanford Linear Accelerator Library

Description: Emphasis is on high energy physics and accelerator technology, electronics, mathematics and computer sciences. Includes special collection of prepublication copies of scientific papers in high energy particle physics, and unclassified technical reports from accelerator laboratories from all over the world as well as from NASA, DOE and other governmental sources.

Contact: Stanford Linear Accelerator Library
PO Box 4349
Stanford, CA 94305
Telephone (415) 854-3300

Union Carbide Corporation K-25 Plant Library

Description: Emphasis is on isotope separation technology, fluid mechanics, chemistry, metallurgy and industrial management.

Contact: Union Carbide Corporation K-25 Plant Library
PO Box P, Nuclear Division
Oak Ridge, TN 37830
Telephone (615) 483-8611

Union Carbide Corporation Y-12 Plant Library

Description: Standard library services are provided to UCC-ND employees in the Oak Ridge Y-12 plant by the Y-12 Technical Library, including a document reference section administered by the Oak Ridge National Laboratory Library. Requests for documents should be directed to the Custodial Plant Records Report Files except for those announced in UCC-ND, which should be directed to the Technical Information Officer. Domestic requests for 2,400 documents and other information are processed each year.

Contact: Union Carbide Corporation Y-12 Plant
PO Box Y, Nuclear Division
Oak Ridge, TN 37830
Telephone (615) 483-8611

DEPARTMENT OF ENERGY CENTERS AND SYSTEMS

ARGONNE NATIONAL LABORATORY

National Energy Software Center

Description: Emphasis is on the Department of Energy programs on reactor design and safety, nuclear physics, structural analysis, engineering studies, basic sciences, and energy technology.

Serves as a central information agency and library for computer software data collections and energy information services. Facilitates software sharing among agency offices and contractors to promote the transfer of technology related to computers.

Department of Energy, NRC and their contractors, government agencies and libraries as wavier list organizations may use the center. Other establishments not eligible for inclusion on the wavier list may choose to participate as subscription fee installations.

Services offered include technical analysis and evaluation. Collects, reviews, tests, distributes and maintains computer software and data packages. Prepares and publishes abstracts and summaries describing programs. Disseminates via a software newsletter information on commercial software, programs and systems developed by other government agencies and requests for particular applications software for the Department of Energy programs.

Contact: Argonne National Laboratory
             National Energy Software Center
             9700 South Cass Avenue
             Argonne, IL 60439
             Telephone (312) 972-2000

Argonne National Laboratory CONCEPT

Description: Computer package developed to provide conceptual capital cost estimates for nuclear and fossil fueled power plants. Details on computer packages available to the public. Reference manual available through NTIS.

Contact: Argonne National Laboratory
             National Energy Software Center
             CONCEPT
             9700 South Cass Avenue
             Argonne, IL 60439
             Telephone (312) 972-2000

BONNEVILLE POWER ADMINISTRATION

Information Center and Library

Description: Emphasis is on hydroelectric generating power systems, marketing of electric power, coordination of river flow and electric power distribution, river basis studies, hydrology, electric utilities materials, test of materials, HVDC, thermal and nuclear power generation, and insulation of HV power lines.

Publishes *Power Outlook, Bonneville Power Administration Annual Report* and annotated bibliographies. Permits on site reference to open file reports.

Contact: Bonneville Power Administration
             Information Center and Library
             PO Box 3621
             Portland, OR 97208
             Telephone (503) 234-3361

BROOKHAVEN NATIONAL LABORATORY

National Center for Analysis of Energy Systems

Description: Emphasis is on energy policy, economic analysis, environmental quality, energy conservation, regional studies of developing countries, energy supplies and technology assessment. Conducts studies of the complex interrelationships between technological, economic, social and environmental factors that influence energy policy.

Contains computerized data bases in energy, economics and the environmental fields. Includes the Energy Model Data Base, County Energy Data Base, and the Brookhaven Energy System Optimization Model.

Answers inquiries and referrals for scientific and technical personnel. Publishes technical reports and journal articles.

Contact: Brookhaven National Laboratory
National Center for Analysis of Energy Systems
Building 475
Upton, Long Island, NY 11973
Telephone (516) 345-2064

National Center for Analysis of Energy Systems, Energy Model Data Base

Description: Documented numeric data for use in energy modeling. Includes energy system process efficiencies, environmental impacts and costs. Answers inquiries free to government agencies and contractors. Publishes Users Manual. Information available on tape and microfiche.

Contact: Brookhaven National Laboratory
National Center for Analysis of Energy Systems
Energy Model Data Base
Upton, Long Island, NY 11973
Telephone (516) 345-2045

National Center for Analysis of Energy Systems, National Nuclear Data Center

Description: Emphasis is on radioactive decay, neutron cross sections, neutrons, nuclear reactions, particles, capture, scattering, absorption and nuclear crossing.

Collects and disseminates data and bibliographies on neutron-induced nuclear reaction and related quantities. These are stored in the three automated library systems and consist of energy and angle-dependent cross sections and resonance parameters.

Maintains the cross-section information storage and retrieval system library in computerized form containing all experimentally measured neutron cross sections. Maintains the Evaluated Nuclear Data File and the Computerized Index to Neutron Data File and the Computerized Index to Neutron Data Bibliography.

Answers inquiries for tabulated data with output on tape, computer card, printout or graphic form for the Department of Energy and Department of Energy contractors. Information is also available for the scientific community. Publishes compilations of experimental and evaluated cross-section data, technical reports, and newsletters.

Contact: National Center for Analysis of Energy Systems
National Nuclear Data Center
Upton, Long Island, NY 11973
Telephone (516) 345-2905
Director: Sol Pearlstein

LAWRENCE BERKELEY LABORATORY

Berkeley Particle Data Group

Description: Emphasis is on elementary particle properties and reaction properties. Content is the compilation of particle physics. Provides referral, bibliography and data compilation, and technical analysis and evaluation to the technical community sponsoring agencies and their contractors.

Publishes *Review of Particle Properties,* LBL 90: An Index of All Documents on Experimental Particle Physics.

Contact: Lawrence Berkeley Laboratory
Berkeley Particle Data Group
Room 308
Building 50
Berkeley, CA 94720
Telephone (415) 843-2740

National Geothermal Information Resource

Description: Emphasis is on physical, chemical exploration, utilization and environmental effects of geothermal science and technology. Provides the preparation of special reviews and data and bibliography searches to Department of Energy and its contractors. Available to other users for nominal charges. Publishes *Compilation of Geothermal Information.*

Contact: Lawrence Berkeley Laboratory
National Geothermal Information Resource
University of California
Berkeley, CA 94720
Telephone (415) 843-2740

Table of Isotopes Project

Description: Produces the *Table of Isotopes* (published by John Wiley and Sons Inc.). Scope includes nuclear data, including properties of radioisotopes, stable nuclei and nuclear level schemes. Answers inquiries from government agencies and the public.

On-line computation of properties useful for nuclear spectroscopy is provided via a dial-up service from standard teletype or equivalent terminal. Requires an account at the LBL computer center. Available to most organizations and government contractors for small fee.

Contact: Lawrence Berkeley Laboratory
            Table of Isotopes Project
            University of California
            Berkeley, CA 94720
            Telephone (415) 843-2740

LAWRENCE LIVERMORE LABORATORY

Analysis and Assessment Group

Description: Studies sources, transport, fate and effects of radionuclides. Constructs models on transport of pollutants from source of receptor. Evaluates dose to man from nuclear and nonnuclear contamination. Also evaluates biological and environmental impacts and the costs of nuclear energy and alternate technologies. Provides referral, data compilation, state of the art studies, technical analysis and evaluation, and technical answers to US government agencies and contractors. Inquiries from other sources are answered as time permits.

Publishes state of the art reviews, data analyses, compilations, and evaluations.

Contact: Lawrence Livermore Laboratory
            Analysis and Assessment Group
            University of California
            Livermore, CA 94550
            Telephone (415) 422-3880

Physical Data Group

Description: Emphasis is on neutron cross sections, photon cross sections, nuclear reactors, reactor shielding calculations, neutrons, nuclear medicine, photonuclear cross sections, nuclear properties, nuclear reactions, and fission.

Provides referral, basic research, consulting, state of the art studies, technical analysis and evaluation, and data compilations to US government agencies and contractors. Inquiries from other sources as time permits.

Contact: Lawrence Livermore Laboratory
            Physical Data Group
            University of California
            Livermore, CA 94550
            Telephone (415) 422-3880

LMFBR FUEL CLADDING INFORMATION CENTER

Description: Provides engineers and scientists data on LMFBR nuclear fuels and cladding materials. It maintains a central data source of materials performance from irradiation tests on experimental mixed oxide fuel elements, and FFTF driver fuel elements. Includes fuels and cladding materials data for LMFBR mixed oxide fuel element development programs. Data for all experimental mixed oxide fuel elements irradiated in the EBR-II are maintained on magnetic tape and microfilm files.

Answers inquiries and provides data compilation. Data is available directly from the computer in the form of tables, plotted curves, and simple statistical analysis. Summaries are prepared for experimental fuel elements irradiated in the EBR-II. Information is available to persons designated by the Department of Energy, Division of Reactor Development and Demonstration.

Users of data include individuals involved in fuel design, modeling, performance predictions, reactor design, proposals and bids, safety and hazard analyses, advisory services, specifications and standards, engineering services and program management.

Contact: LMFBR Fuel Cladding Information Center
Westinghouse Hanford Company
Hanford Engineering Development Laboratory
PO Box 1970
Richland, WA 19352
Telephone (509) 942-3284

NEVADA OPERATIONS OFFICE

Nevada Applied Ecology Information Center

Description: Concerned with bioenvironmental data for the nuclear testing site. Contains government data on radiation dose, environmental conditions of chemical isotopes, organisms used in research, route of intake, particle size and effects.

Analyzes data pertinent to the scope of the center, and offers bibliographic services. Upon request consults with members of the public, industry and scientific community. Machine searchable data bases may be accessed through the Ecology Information Center, Oak Ridge National Laboratory at Oak Ridge TN.

Contact: Nevada Operations Office
Nevada Applied Ecology Information Center
PO Box 14100
Las Vegas, NV 89114
Telephone (702) 734-3194

OAK RIDGE TENNESSEE INFORMATION CENTERS

Technical Information Center at Oak Ridge, Tennessee

Description: Emphasis is on nuclear science, power reactor, licensing and regulations, energy policy, coal technology, solar energy, geothermal, oil shales, magnetohydrodynamics, conservation, electric power, thermonuclear power, environment and safety and basic research and development.

TIC is the collection processing and distribution point for scientific and technical information generated by the Department of Energy programs. It is TIC's responsibility to ensure that the Department of Energy research is reported.

Acquires and evaluates energy related scientific and technical literature from around the world. Inputs descriptive cataloging, abstracts, and subject indexing of this literature for the computerized energy data base. Searches this data either by batch (RESPONSA) or on line RECON. RECON is the Department of Energy computerized on-line interactive storage and retrieval system. It is designed to permit scientists, librarians, and information specialists to obtain direct and fast access to bibliographies and records. The Technical Information Center provides total input and evaluation.

Data bases available through DOE RECON system:

Nuclear Science Abstracts — Citations from the journal.

Energy Data Base EISO — Includes the use, generation and distribution on reported movements of crude oil.

Engineering Index — Contains citations from journals, publications of engineering organizations and selected government reports.

Energy R&D Projects — Contains projects and proposed work in energy research by private and governmental research institutes.

Nuclear Safety Information File — Contains a wide variety of citations and data sources.

DOE Energy Data Base — Encompasses all areas of related information.

Nuclear Structure Reference — Created by Nuclear Data Project personnel.

Toxic Materials Data Base — Includes effects on the environment of numerous toxic substances.

Water Resources Abstracts — Abstracts on groundwater hydrology and the prediction of radionuclide migration in the ground.

Output for the DOE Energy Data Base is as follows:

Department of Energy Research Abstracts — Provides coverage of nonnuclear and nuclear energy scientific reports, patents, journal articles, conference papers, mongraphs originated by the Department of Energy, laboratories, energy centers and contractors.

Fossil Energy Update — Current announcements of publications covering fossil energy R&D issued by the Department of Energy.

Geothermal Energy Update — Current announcements of publications covering the geothermal energy R&D field.

Solar Energy Update — Current announcements of publications covering solar energy R&D.

Energy Abstracts for Policy Analysis — Provides abstracting and indexing coverage of selected available nontechnical literature contributing to energy related analysis and evaluation. The thrust is toward policy issues, economics, supply and demand, and forecasting of major potential energy sources.

Nuclear Safety Data — Bibliographies, handbooks and symposium proceedings.

The Technical Information Center supplies coverage of US literature on atomic energy to IAEA's International Nuclear Information System. Provides reference, referral and technical answers to the Department of Energy, contractors, government agencies, industry and individuals. Publications are available through the Government Printing Office and NTIS in paper form and microfiche. Maintains a centralized film library and loan service. Films and education materials available from TIC. TIC has a remote copier which can be used to receive messages from users who have compatible equipment.

Contact: Department of Energy
Technical Information Center
PO Box 62
Oak Ridge, TN 37830
Telephone (615) 483-8611

Information Center Complex

Description: Seven major types of services are supplied to users. These services include bibliographic, reference, inventories of current research projects, factual information, numerical data organization of collected materials and assessment of information.

Subject areas include air quality, animal physiology, chlorination effects, coal conversion effects, coal processing technology, drug metabolism, ecological research, energy analysis, energy conservation, energy R&D, environmental exposure hazards, environmental monitoring, environmental sciences, research, environmental standards and criteria, environmental toxicology, environmental transport of chemicals, genetics research, microbiology, environmental modeling, mutagenesis research, pesticides, pharmacology, physiology, plant physiology, thermal effluents, toxicology, wastewater treatment and water quality.

Component Centers

Health and Environmental Studies Program

Description: Emphasis is on toxicology, pharmacology, biomedicine, environments, pollution, chemicals, biological contamination, and toxicity. Provides bibliography and data compilation, literature surveys, state of the art reviews, and referral to the scientific and technical community. Publishes annotated literature reviews and state of the art reviews.

Contact: Oak Ridge National Laboratory
Information Center Complex
Oak Ridge, TN 37830
Telephone (615) 483-8511, extension 1433

Biomedical Sciences

Description: BIOSCI component interactive groups represent a multidisciplinary cross section in the life sciences. Component groups include Environmental Mutagen Information Center, Environmental Teratology Information Center, Toxicology Data Bank and the Toxicology Information Response Center.

Provides state of the art reviews, data extraction for a computerized surrogate chemicals handbook file, collection, analysis and computer storage of chemically induced mutagen and teratogen information and a broad based toxicology information gathering and analysis response service. These services are provided to sponsoring agencies, contractors and others.

Publishes bibliographies, topical overviews, state of the art review, and monographs. These are published as ORNL reports and as articles in the peer reviewed scientific literature.

Contact: Oak Ridge National Laboratory
Information Center Complex
Biomedical Sciences
PO Box X
Building 7509
Oak Ridge, TN 37830
Telephone (615) 483-8611

Toxicology Data Bank —

Description: Provides information on toxic compounds including physical and chemical properties, and lethal dose values. Provides information retrieval, referral, data compilation, indexing, technical and evaluation, and data bases to the public for an hourly fee.

Contact: Oak Ridge National Laboratory
Information Center Complex
Toxicology Data Bank
PO Box X
Building 7503
Oak Ridge, TN 37830
Telephone (615) 483-8611
Director: Jack Tobler

Environmental Mutagen Information Center —

Description: Emphasis is on mutagens, mutations, chromosomes, deoxyribonucleic acids, ribonucleic acids, nucleic acids, mitosis, meiosis, genetics.

Provides bibliographic compilations, technical answers, referral and literature surveys. Information provided to the public via NLM's on-line computer system.

Publishes *Surveys of Chemical Mutagenesis Literature, Bibliography of the Effects of Chemicals on Germ Cells, Chemical Mutagenesis Studies in Plants.* Available through NTIS.

Contact: Oak Ridge National Laboratory
Information Center Complex
Environmental Mutagen Information Center
PO Box X
Oak Ridge, TN 37830
Telephone (615) 483-8611
Director: John Wasson

Toxicology Information Response Center —

Description: Emphasis is on toxicology, toxicity, environments, chemicals, industrial medicine and pharmacology. Provides bibliography compilation, state of the art reviews, technical analyses, evaluation and answers to the public and scientific personnel. Publishes bibliographies, books, science journals, available through NTIS.

Contact: Oak Ridge National Laboratory
Information Center Complex
Toxicology Information Response Center
PO Box X
Oak Ridge, TN 37830
Telephone (615) 483-8611
Director: Helga Gerstner

Environmental Teratology Information Center —

Description: Information on data relating to environmental teratology. Data available on animals and chemical testing. ETIC data base is available for on-line searching.

Contact: Oak Ridge National Laboratory
Information Center Complex
PO Box X
Oak Ridge, TN 37830
Telephone (615) 483-8611
Director: J.S. Wasson

Energy and Environmental Sciences

Ecological Sciences Information Center —

Description: Center provides assessment of the environmental impact of both nuclear and fossil energy. Computerized information files are compiled on the environmental impact of cooling electric generating stations. Subjects related to cooling include effects of temperature on chlorine and other chemicals, their impingement and entrainment.

Information support is provided to the National Uranium Resource Evaluation Project with a computer searchable file of annotated references to the geochemistry and geophysics of uranium. Transport of uranium and thorium in the environment as related to the thorium fuel cycle is the subject of a data base, annotated bibliography and critical review.

Provides abstracting, bibliography compilations, state of the art reviews, indexing, literature surveys, and referral to the public, agencies, and their contractors. Publishes bibliographies that are available from NTIS.

Contact: Oak Ridge National Laboratory
Information Center Complex
Ecological Sciences Information Center
PO Box X
Oak Ridge, TN 37830
Telephone (615) 483-8611
Director: Helen Fuderer

Energy Research and Development Inventory —

Description: Computerized file containing descriptions of current energy related research done or sponsored in the U.S. Includes information on the following:

(1) energy sources—fossil fuels, nuclear, and unconventional;
(2) electric power generation, transmission, distribution and storage;
(3) energy uses and conservation—heating and cooling, industrial processes, transportation, and agriculture;
(4) economic and legal aspects; and
(5) environmental and health effects.

Information is also provided on exploration, mining, processing, resources and reserve studies, and any basic or applied research and engineering development.

Projects are arranged by subject categories and consist of title, research institution, sponsor, principal investigator, project duration, funding level, description of research, number of technical personnel assigned to the project, and type of research publications.

Provides data compilation, technical analysis and evaluation, indexing, referral, abstracting, and technical answers. Answers inquiries as time and money permit. Some services free, others on a cost recovery charge.

Publishes *Inventory of Current Research and Development,* 1972, 1973, January 1974, 1975, and January 1976. New inventories are being prepared.

Contact: Oak Ridge National Laboratory
                  Energy Research and Development Inventory
                  PO Box X
                  Oak Ridge, TN 37830
                  Telephone (615) 483-8611

Energy and Environmental Response Center —

Description: Capabilities range broadly across the environmental damage
                  and control spectrum, from energy technologies to hazardous
                  substances. Subject areas include environments, ecology, fossil
                  fuels, trace elements, coal conversion, oil shales, organic mate-
                  rials, control, and public health pollution.

                  Contains environmental data bases and in-house collections on
                  environmental, health and control data of the emerging energy
                  technologies. The Toxic Materials Information Center and the
                  Environmental Response Center and other projects have been
                  clustered into the ERC.

                  Provides bibliographic compilation, state of the art reviews,
                  technical analysis and evaluation, technical answers, and refer-
                  rals. Available to the public with some services free, while oth-
                  ers operate on cost recovery charges. Publishes abstract jour-
                  nals, newsletters, and topical reviews.

Contact: Oak Ridge National Laboratory
                  Information Center Complex
                  Energy and Environmental Response Center
                  PO Box X
                  Oak Ridge, TN 37830
                  Telephone (615) 483-8611
                  Director: D.J. Wilkes

Oak Ridge Laboratories (Research and Technical Centers)

Nuclear Data Project

Description: Emphasis is on nuclear structure, nuclear binding energy, nu-
                  clear forces, nuclear properties, nuclear energy labels, nuclear
                  models, and nuclear physics.

                  The project maintains a complete computer indexed library of
                  published works in experimental nuclear physics. The center
                  has a computer based system for evaluated nuclear structure
                  data.

                  Provides on request individual estimates of the current best
                  available values of nuclear level or decay projects. Provides ref-
                  erence lists, and answers inquiries.

                  Publishes Nuclear Data Sheets (published by Academic Press).
                  Reference and key word lists are available from DOE RECON
                  in the nuclear structure reference field.

Contact: Oak Ridge Laboratories
Nuclear Data Project
PO Box X
Oak Ridge, TN 37830
Telephone (615) 483-8611
Director: E.B. EwBank

Nuclear Safety Information Center

Description: Covers all aspects of nuclear safety, such as general criteria, analysis and operating systems, environmental surveys, monitoring, siting and containment of facilities, transporting and handling of radioactive materials, reactor transients, kinetics and stability, nuclear instrumentation and control.

Other engineering safety features included are emergency power systems, emergency core cooling systems, filter systems, release and transport of fission products, accident analyses and risk assessment.

Contains technical information involved in the licensing of nuclear facilities and operational data relating to their safe operation. NSIC information file contains complete bibliographies, data abstracts and keywords.

Provides abstracting, bibliography and data compilation, indexing, literature surveys, state of the art reviews, technical analysis and evaluation, referral, and computer printouts to government agencies, contractors, research and educational institutions. Others may use NSIC services at cost recovery basis.

Publishes state of the art reports, technical progress reviews, *Nuclear Safety* and bibliographies.

Contact: Oak Ridge National Laboratory
Nuclear Safety Information Center
PO Box X
Oak Ridge, TN 37830
Telephone (615) 483-8611
Director: William Cottrell

Radiation Shielding Information Center

Description: Provides data on radiation interaction, transport, and shielding information. Serves as a national technology resource, collecting, organizing, evaluating, and disseminating information related to radiation from reactor, radioisotopes, weapons, accelerators, and to that occurring in space.

RSIC collects, examines, packages, and disseminates complex digital computer codes, evaluated cross-section data sets, multigroup data libraries, radiation environment data, and benchmark problems for use in shielding calculations. The center answers technical inquiries with the assistance of the computerized storage and retrieval information system.

Publishes newsletter, literature accession lists, state of the art reviews, bibliographies and abstracts of computer code and data packages.

Contact: Oak Ridge National Laboratory
            Radiation Shielding Information Center
            PO Box X
            Oak Ridge, TN 37830
            Telephone (615) 483-8611

Biomedical Computing Technology Information Center

Description: Provides a national computing technology resource to clinical medical practice and to biomedical research and development. Assesses the state of the art fostering the exchange of computing technology and promotes the advancement of the state of the art. Answers all scientific and technical inquiries. Personnel associated with the sponsors' interests are served free of charge.

Publishes *Directory of Computer Users in Nuclear Medicine,* abstracts of the computer code and data packages, handbooks, and newsletters. Publications are available through NTIS.

Contact: Oak Ridge National Laboratory
            Biomedical Computing Technology Information Center
            PO Box X
            Oak Ridge, TN 37830
            Telephone (615) 483-8611

Controlled Fusion Atomic Data Center

Description: Produces data on collisions involving charged and neutral particles with gases and surface which are directly related to controlled thermonuclear research.

Provides bibliography and data compilations, state of the art reviews to government agencies, contractors, research and educational institutions and industry. The center is exempt from DOE-NTIS charging policy.

Publishes *Atomic Molecular Collision Cross Sections of Interest to Controlled Thermonuclear Research,* plus a newsletter.

Contact: Oak Ridge National Laboratory
            Controlled Fusion Atomic Data Center
            PO Box X
            Oak Ridge, TN 37830
            Telephone (615) 483-8611

Mechanical Properties Data Center

Description: Information is provided on the mechanical properties of structural metals/alloys. Provides data compilation, literature surveys, technical analysis and evaluation, and referral. Publishes *Aerospace Structural Metals Handbook.*

Contact: Oak Ridge National Laboratory
                Mechanical Properties Data Center
                PO Box X
                Oak Ridge, TN 37830
                Telephone (615) 483-8611

Eco Systems Analysis Data Center

Description: Provides a broad array of numeric data concerning aquatic and
                terrestrial information.

Contact: Oak Ridge National Laboratory
                Eco Systems Analysis Data Center
                PO Box X
                Oak Ridge, TN 37830
                Telephone (615) 483-8611
                Julie Watta

Geoecology Data Base

Description: Provides numeric data concentrating on environmental and eco-
                logical information.

Contact: Oak Ridge National Laboratory
                Geoecology Data Base
                PO Box X
                Oak Ridge, TN 37830
                Telephone (615) 483-8611
                Richard Olsen

Research Materials Information Center

Description: Emphasis is on the availability, preparation, crystal growth,
                and the physical, optical, magnetic, and electrical properties
                of high purity inorganic research materials.

                Provides bibliography and data compilations, referrals, litera-
                ture surveys, state of the art studies, and technical answers to
                qualified researchers on an information exchange basis.

                Publishes solid state physics literature guides, *Directory of
                Solid State Materials Production and Research* and special
                bibliographies.

Contact: Oak Ridge National Laboratory
                Research Materials Information Center
                PO Box X
                Oak Ridge, TN 37830
                Telephone (615) 483-8611
                Director: T.F. Connolly

Information Center for Energy Safety

Description: Disseminates safety information essential to the development
                and use of several nonnuclear forms. Concerned with the de-
                sign, construction and operation of various energy systems.

Energy safety is related to the following energy technologies: solar, coal, coal conversion and utilization, energy and source chemicals as obtained by the conversion of coal, oil and shale, MHD, thermonuclear, geothermal, electrical energy systems and advanced systems.

Provides answers to technical inquiries, state of the art reviews, and periodic dissemination of information to government agencies. Others will be afforded free service where time and budget permit. Publishes monthly material in National Safety Council R&D newsletter.

Contact: Oak Ridge National Laboratory
Information Center for Energy Safety
PO Box X
Oak Ridge, TN 37830
Telephone (615) 483-8611

Union Carbide Nuclear Division—Orlook System

Description: Oak Ridge National Laboratory has an information retrieval system operated by Union Carbide. Subject areas include coal technology, nuclear reactors, radiation shieldings and ecology. Publishes journals, reports and engineering data.

Contact: Union Carbide Nuclear Division
Orlook System
Building 4500 s
PO Box X
Oak Ridge, TN 37830
Telephone (615) 483-8611, extension 3-609

REGIONAL ENERGY/ENVIRONMENT INFORMATION CENTERS

Southern Energy/Environmental Information Center

Description: Clearinghouse for energy and environmental information to the sixteen-state southeastern region. In addition to its own facilities, it utilizes the facilities of Georgia Tech Library.

Contact: Southern Energy/Environmental Information Center
1 Exchange Place
Suite 1150
2300 Peachford Road
Atlanta, GA 30338
Telephone (404) 458-6871

Conservation Library

Description: Clearinghouse for energy and environmental information to the ten-state Rocky Mountain Plains region. Funded jointly by DOE and EPA. Receives cooperative assistance from the Department of Interior, U.S. Forest Services, Department of Commerce and HEW.

Contact: Conservation Library
                Denver Public Library
                1375 Broadway
                Denver, CO 80203
                Telephone (303) 837-5994

Mid-American Solar Energy Complex (under development)

Description: Areas of interest include applications, usage, commercializa-
                tion, conservation in solar applications. Answers inquiries, con-
                ducts seminars and workshops. Provides on site usage of the li-
                brary collection. Holdings include books, journals, reports,
                patents, directories, and resource data.

Contact: Mid-American Solar Energy Complex
                1256 Trapp Road
                Eagan, MN 55121
                Telephone (612) 452-5300

Northeast Solar Energy Center (under development)

Description: Areas of interest include applications, usage, commercializa-
                tion research. Answers inquiries, and conducts computerized
                information searches. Holdings include books, journals, reports
                and directories. Resource data and industry activity files avail-
                able.

Contact: Northeast Solar Energy Center
                70 Memorial Drive
                Cambridge, MA 02142
                Telephone (617) 661-3500

Western Regional Solar Energy Center

Description: Provides unique western applications of solar energy, conserva-
                tion relating to solar applications. Answers inquiries, sponsors
                workshops, and provides technical assistance.

Contact: Western Regional Solar Energy Center
                c/o Bonneville Power Administration
                PO Box 3621
                Portland, OR 92708

Solar Energy Research Institute

Description: SERI is DOE's lead institute for solar research development
                and demonstration. It is operated by Midwest Research Insti-
                tute in Golden, Colorado under DOE contract.

                SERI's mission is to undertake principal responsibility for the
                management and performance of RD&D programs and proj-
                ects; provide planning support to DOE on national solar energy
                policies, program plans and strategies; maintain a capability for
                market analysis and assessment of institutional barriers to solar
                technologies on a national and international basis; collect and
                distribute solar energy information and conduct education and
                training in the application of this information.

SERI is authorized to regional, state and local governments, federal agencies, foreign governments, private sector and non-government entities.

Contact: Library
Midwest Research Institute
1536 Cole Boulevard
Golden, CO 80401

or the Department of Energy's Office of Assistant Secretary for Energy Technologies.

OTHER DOE INFORMATION CENTERS AND SYSTEMS

Power Information Center

Description: The Center is a DOD/NASA/NSF/DOE information center. Subject areas include power energy conversion, energy storage, power supplies, nuclear energy, solar energy, power plants, electric power production, electrochemistry, electrostatics, electrostatic generators, and electromagnetism.

Provides referral R&D, project data compilation, indexing, technical analysis and evaluation to subscribers and Interagency Advanced Power GP.

Publishes technical project briefs on advanced nonpropulsive power field, and proceedings of conferences.

Contact: Power Information Center
University City Science Center 3624
Philadelphia, PA 19104
Telephone (215) 382-8683

Project Information Systems

Contracts Information System

Description: Centralized data base that collects and processes contract and procurement data. Input comes from headquarters, field offices and energy research centers. Contract data is for active on-going contracts for $10,000 or more.

Information given on contracts includes name of company or individuals that received contract, description of contract, city, state, award amount and completion date. It is reported by budget and reporting number.

Eight listings are available and may be ordered individually or in one package. Listings are as follows: by state, by type of work, information on architectural and engineering contracts, information on research and development contracts, information on materials contracts, information on supply contracts, information on contracts for rents and utilities and information on operating contracts and other services.

Contact: Department of Energy
             Contracts Information System
             Division of Procurement
             C 167
             Washington, DC 20545
             Telephone (301) 353-3202

Research Projects Information System

Description: This is a management information system that integrates con-
              tractual, budgetary, financial, and technical information in one
              central data base on environmental safety. Some proprietary in-
              formation internal only. Other output available to the public
              upon request. Publishes computer reports.

Contact: Department of Energy
              Office of Program Coordination
              20 Massachusetts Avenue, NW
              Washington, DC 20545
              Telephone (202) 353-3541

Radiation Chemistry Data Center

Description: The center is an NBS/DOE sponsored information analysis cen-
              ter. Subject areas include radiation chemistry, ionizing radia-
              tion, irradiation, electrons, protons, alpha particles, beta par-
              ticles, deuterons, chemical reactions, chemical properties, phys-
              ical chemistry, and radiation.

              Collects and indexes literature on radiation chemistry and re-
              lated topics. Maintains a computerized bibliographic data base
              for providing bibliographies, retrospective searches and current
              awareness services.

              Compiles kinetic data on chemical reactions brought about by
              ionizing radiation, and other properties of irradiated systems.
              Publishes compilations and critical reviews of the data. Empha-
              sis is on kinetic and spectroscopic data for transients and radia-
              tion effects on chemical systems.

              Provides bibliography and data compilation, indexing, literature
              surveys, and referral to all professional scientific and technical
              individuals. Information on charges available.

              Publishes *Biweekly List of Papers on Radiation Chemistry,*
              data compilations and critical reviews on the radiolysis of se-
              lected compounds, rate data for transients in solution, and
              other properties of irradiated systems in the NSRDS-NBS ser-
              ies.

Contact: Radiation Chemistry Data Center
              Radiation Laboratory
              University of Notre Dame
              Notre Dame, IN 46556
              Telephone (219) 283-6527

Rare Earth Information Center

Description: Concerned with the metallurgy and solid state physics of the rare earth metals, intermetallic compounds and alloys, the analytical, inorganic and physical chemistry, ceramics, technology, geochemistry, and the toxicity of the rare earth elements compounds. Emphasis is on the physical metallurgy and solid state physics of the metals and their alloys.

Provides references, referrals, surveys and in-depth analyses on a cost recovery basis. Maintains a file of journal articles, reports, books and translations concerned with the rare earths. Files are accessible for on site use by prior arrangements. Publishes reviews, bibliographies and compilations and RIC news.

Contact: Rare Earth Information Center
Energy and Mineral Resources Research Institute
Iowa State University
Ames, IA 50011
Telephone (515) 294-2272

ENERGY INFORMATION ADMINISTRATION

Energy Information Administration is part of the Department of Energy. EIA carries out a central comprehensive and unified energy data and information program which collects, evaluates, assembles, analyzes, and disseminates data and information relevant to energy resources, reserves, production, demand and technology.

Publishes many publications in the energy field. A list of publications is available from EIS. Publications may be ordered from EIA, GPO, and NTIS. Microfiche of 1978 EIA publications will be available.

NATIONAL ENERGY INFORMATION CENTER

Description: Source of information on energy and national data bases. Expertise on energy sources and applications. Emphasis is on energy supply and demand, energy economics, oil recovery, offshore drilling, oil shale, power sources, nonconventional power systems, hydroelectric power generation, energy conversion, energy resources, energy storage, energy consumption and conservation.

Holdings in print form, microform and automated data bases. On line search available.

OFFICE OF ENERGY DATA AND INTERPRETATION

Description: Maintains and provides a capacity for ready access to data elements and data bases not generally published but used by analysts, policymakers and other users. Emphasis is on fossil fuel supply for the U.S. Includes coal, crude oil, coke, petroleum products, natural gas, oil shale, peat, lebium and hydrogen, fuel production and consumption.

Answers inquiries, provides magnetic tape service and distributes some publications. Others are sold by GPO. Provides computerized data.

Contact: Energy Information Administration
Office of Energy Information Services
1726 M Street, NW
Washington, DC 20241
Telephone (202) 634-5602

National Energy Information Center
1726 M Street, NW
Washington, DC 20241
Telephone (202) 634-5612

Office of Energy Data and Interpretation
2401 E Street, NW
Room 619
Washington, DC 20241
Telephone (202) 634-1047

Department of Agriculture

14th Street and Independence Avenue SW
Washington, DC 20250
Locator (202) 655-4000   Public Affairs (202) 447-2791

NATIONAL AGRICULTURAL LIBRARY

Contains comprehensive materials on agricultural research. Publications include agricultural research. Publications include agriculture on-line access bibliography.

AGRICOLA

Description: Provides on-line bibliographic search and retrieval service to provide information on publications in the National Agricultural Library to scientists and researchers.

Monthly tapes are for sale. Data base can be queried on site at NAL.

Contact: National Agricultural Library
10301 Baltimore Boulevard
Beltsville, MD 20705
Telephone (301) 344-3755 or (301) 344-3756

Department of Commerce

14th Street Between E Street and Constitution Avenue NW
Washington, DC 20230
Locator (202) 377-2000   Public Affairs (202) 377-4901

NATIONAL TECHNICAL INFORMATION SERVICE (NTIS)

NTIS is a central pemanent source of specialized information in the business and scientific fields. Bibliographies, information services and research reports are described below.

NTIS BIBLIOGRAPHIC DATA FILE

Description: Contains all the research summaries and other data and analyses. Most items have full bibliographic citations, and they may be used to create a wide variety of information products. Available on magnetic tape and may be leased annually. Lease fees are negotiated. Subscribers may search by research report, title, personal or corporate author, accession or contract number by subject using key words. Basic lease fee is $4,000 annually plus a negotiated use charge.

The following products are produced from the bibliographic data file.

Government Reports Announcements and Index

Description: Summaries of government research are published in one biweekly volume with an index by subject, personal and corporate author, government contract and report/accession numbers.

Weekly Government Abstracts

Description: Newsletters with timely research summaries within two weeks of their receipt by NTIS from the originating agencies. Coverage is in 26 areas of government research. Energy WGA reports cover energy sources, use, supply, power, heat generation, energy conversion and storage, energy transmission, fuel conversion processes, energy policies, regulations, and studies.

NTIS Directory of Computerized Data Files
(Out of stock—pending revision)

Published Searches

Description: Printed searches published in response to demand to NTIS's anticipation of wide interest in a field. Subjects include aeronautics, aerodynamics, astronomy and astrophysics, atmospheric sciences, business and economics, biomedical, technology and engineering, chemistry, energy, environment, pollution and control, materials sciences, nuclear science and technology, ocean technology, technology transfer, urban and regional technology and development. Each research summary includes title of full report, author, corporate or government source, pages, price and instructions for ordering full text.

Custom Searches (NTISearch)

Description: Provides instant access to reports on completed U.S. government research analysis and technical innovations. Reports average 250 words. Delivery time is usually 21 days. Cost is $100 for up to 100 research summaries.

SRIM

Description: Contains complete research reports, not just abstracts, in the subject areas selected. Available in microfiche only in subjects selected. There are 500 subject categories and 200,000 descriptive terms. It is possible to order all of any individual government agency or other organization research reports entering the NTIS system.

Tech Notes

Description: Pulls together into a single biweekly package one-page summaries on new applications for technology as developed by Federal agencies and their contractors. Also included in the packages are selected technology for licensing. Subject areas include computers, electrotechnology, energy, engineering, life sciences, machinery, materials, manufacturing, ordnance and testing and instrumentation. Users may subscribe to any one category or a combination.

ENERGY PUBLICATIONS

Description: Energy information is available through publications and in some cases on a subscription basis.

Energy—A Continuing Bibliography with Indexes

Description: Introduced by NASA and is published quarterly. Coverage includes regional, national and international energy systems, R&D on fuels and other sources of energy, energy conversion, transport, transmission, distribution and storage with special emphasis on the use of hydrogen and solar energy.

Monthly Petroleum Statistics Report

Description: Includes statistics on refinery operations, refinery production, petroleum products, primary stocks of crude oil and petroleum products and imports of crude oil, unfinished oils and petroleum products. Available on a subscription basis.

Fusion Energy Update

Description: This monthly DOE publication abstracts and indexes current scientific and technical reports, journal articles, conference papers and proceedings for all sources of fusion energy. Available monthly.

Solar Energy Update

Description: Announces research, development and demonstration information from all sources. It abstracts and indexes reports, journal articles, conference proceedings, patents, theses, and monographs. Available monthly.

Geothermal Energy Update

Description: Contains references to reports, journal articles, conference proceedings, patents, theses, and monographs. Available monthly.

Energy Conservation Update

Description: Provides abstracts and an index to the latest studies of energy conservation worldwide. Covers a broad spectrum from transportation and industrial energy savings to the latest research dealing with techniques for residential and commercial heating, lighting, and hot water conservation. Available monthly.

Fossil Energy Update

Description: Abstracts information in the subject areas such as coal, petroleum, natural gas, oil shale, hydrogen production, hydrocarbon and alcohol fuels, electric power engineering and magnetohydrodynamic generators. Available monthly.

Directory of Computer Software Applications: Energy

Description: Presents abstracts of energy-related reports and computer programs developed from federally sponsored research. The abstracts describe in detail the computer software available in fossil, solar, nuclear, geothermal, ocean thermal and other energy areas. This directory is the first in a series. Areas under consideration for the future include marine engineering, mathematics and astronomy and astrophysics.

Energy SOS

Description: Contains full text of every printed report published by NTIS in the field of energy. Subjects include energy sources, energy use, supply and demand, power and heat generation, energy conversion and storage, energy transmission, fuel conversion processes, policies, regulations and studies, engines and fuels.

Energy Microthesaurus—A Hierarchical List of Indexing Terms Used by NTIS

Description: Information on energy keyword descriptors, and information sources. This microthesaurus will assist those planning to produce and index vocabularies as well as those who search the NTIS Bibliographic Data File. Another new microthesaurus produced by NTIS is Environmental Microthesaurus—A Hierarchical List of Indexing Terms Used by NTIS. This thesaurus is a hierarchical list of environmental indexing terms used by NTIS.

Reports on Energy Information Reported to Congress

Description: The Office of Data and Analysis in the DOE reports to Congress the status of international energy exploration, consumption, storage, production and transportation. Issued quarterly.

Monthly Energy Review

Description: This publication is the principal communications medium for EIA and incorporates the energy information previously published in the PIMS Monthly Petroleum Report, the supplements to PIMS and Monthly Energy Indicators. The major parts are an overview summarizing events of the previous month and sections on crude oil and refined petroleum products, natural gas, coal, nuclear power, electric utilities, consumption, resource development.

An Inexpensive Economical Solar Heating System for Homes

Description: This publication is produced by NASA and gives instructions for building a $2000 solar heating system to supplement forced warm air heating.

Petroleum Market Shares—Refined Petroleum Products

Description: A continuing series of reports of monitored monthly changes in the refiner sales distribution and the retail market shares of selected refined petroleum products.

Nuclear Regulatory Commission Reports and Periodicals

Nuclear Regulatory Commission Issuances

Description: Monthly publication with semiannual indexes of the NRC. It comprises a compilation of adjudicatory decisions and other issuances of the commission's Atomic Safety and Licensing Appeal Boards and the Atomic Safety and Licensing Boards.

Standard Review Plan

Description: A safety review of applications to build and operate lightwater cooled nuclear power reactors. Describes the various safety related technical areas.

Water Reactor Safety Research Status Summary Report

Description: Status summary report that reviews the safety research program from a management point of view.

Operating Units Status Report

Description: Monthly report on all of the licensed nuclear power units in the U.S.

Construction Status of Nuclear Power Plants

Description: Information on the monitoring of nuclear power plant construction.

Licensee Contractor and Vendor Inspection Status Report

Description: Includes information on the total nuclear inspection activity as verified, inspected or audited by the licensee, his contractors, vendors and NRC.

DOE's Unclassified Data on Nuclear Operations and Research

Description: These are technical reports, critical reviews, and conference papers. Reports are in the NTIS newsletters and journals. Sold in paper copy and microfiche. Issued irregularly.

GOVERNMENT-OWNED PATENT DATA

Description: Information on DOE government-owned patents is available from NTIS through the newsletter Government Inventions for Licensing. These inventions come out of government laboratories and also contractor inventions to which the government has title. The most promising inventions are summarized in Selected Technology for Licensing.

Copies of the pending patent applications are sold in paper and microfiche. Where inventions have not been assigned to the Department of Commerce, NTIS refers prospective licenses to the appropriate licensing agencies. These will normally be non-exclusive royalty-free licenses, but in some instances may be exclusive or royalty-bearing.

FOREIGN TECHNOLOGY AND TRANSLATIONS

Description: Information and services that are available through NTIS that can be of assistance in utilizing and understanding foreign technical data.

Foreign Technology Information

Soviet Information

Description: NTIS has negotiated the rights to publish and sell English translations of 6 copyrighted Soviet scientific and technical journals as well as selected articles from journals and selected Soviet books.

Index to the Daily Report—People's Republic of China

Description: The Daily Report—People's Republic of China is issued by the Foreign Broadcast Information Service. Researchers can analyze current events, identify trends, locate crop damage and petroleum production, from this daily report. The index is designed to help scientists and researchers find this information more efficiently.

Applications of Modern Technology to International Development

Description: There are 18 cooperating agencies combining their resources in a technical information network of mutual benefits. AID and NTIS support this network by making available specially selected technical information. The monthly newsletter describes new technical reports of particular interest to the cooperating agencies in the various countries.

ESDU Data Items

Description: A collection of evaluated engineering design data is available through NTIS by agreement with Engineering Sciences Data Unit in London. The basic ESDU package is the Data Item, a set of looseleaf sheets devoted to a single topic and containing graphical data, equations and tables, definitions and terminology, explanatory matter and worked examples.

Information Services on Research in Progress—A Worldwide Inventory

Description: A directory that is the first worldwide compilation of systems and services which provide information on scientific research projects in progress. It presents data on 179 existing and emerging centers in 53 countries.

Foreign Translation Services

Special Foreign Currency Science Information Program

Description: NSF coordinated the Special Foreign Currency Science Information Program and translated foreign R&D reports. Research scientists in government agencies select the material to be translated under the advice of scientists, academic institutions and professional societies. Translations are announced by NTIS in the WGA and Government Reports Announcement and Indexes.

Joint Publications Research Service

Description: JPRS translates and abstracts foreign language political and technical media for Federal agencies. Most JPRS reports are concerned with publications in communist countries though materials from all nations may be translated. About half of the reports are in the scientific and technical fields. An index to JPRS translations is available from the Micro Photo Division of Bell & Howell, Old Mansfield Road, Wooster OH 44691. It is called the TRANSDEX Index.

Contact: JPRS
                1000N Glebe Rd.
                Arlington, VA 22201
                Telephone (703) 841-1050

ORDER INFORMATION FOR NTIS PUBLICATIONS

Regular Service

Description: Send order form and payment for order to NTIS. Order will be sent with regular mail delivery or priority mail delivery can be arranged for a slightly higher amount. Orders may be picked up and paid for either in Springfield, VA or Washington, DC.

Premium Service

Description: A new day and night toll free telephone ordering procedure ensuring priority order processing to NTIS Deposit Account or American Express Card. All deposit account and American Express card customers receive premium service with identification number by which they may place telephone orders at any time.

Deposit Account

Description: Send $25.00 or more to cover your first order. Thereafter keep at least $25.00 deposit or enough to cover 2 months charges. When the account is opened, preaddressed order forms are sent to special order and simplify accounting and recording of tax deductible expenses.

Rush Handling

Description: Guarantees that a particular order will be filled within 24 hours of its receipt. Accepted from customers with NTIS deposit accounts or American Express cards. May be placed by telephone, telegram, telex, telecopier or customers in person, not by mail. Rush handling for delivery to customers by priority mail is $10.00 for each item ordered. Rush handling pickup in Springfield, VA or Washington, DC costs $6.00 for each item ordered.

Washington DC Bookstore

Description: NTIS has retail sales locations in the Washington, DC area. In

Washington DC, the NTIS Information Center and Bookstore is in the Pennsylvania Building, Suite 620, 425 13th Street NW (202) 724-3382. The bookstore contains best sellers off the shelf, Government Reports Announcements, Weekly Government Abstracts, NTISearch Catalog.

Contact: For customer services

NTIS
5285 Port Royal Road
Springfield, VA 22161
Telephone (202) 724-3509 or (703) 557-4600

PATENT OFFICE

PATENT SEARCH FILES

Description: System designed to provide a collection of U.S. and foreign patents to be used by patent examiners, patent attorneys, and inventors in search of prior information in relation to filing or prosecuting patent applications, by individuals seeking a specific patent and by the general public. Publications are available through GPO and include

General Information Concerning Patents
Annual Indexes
Patent Official Gazette
Manual of Patent Examining Procedure
Manual Classification of Patents and Inventions

The search room is open to the public and is located at the Patent and Trademark Office. Copies of the specifications and drawings on all patents are available.

Contact: Patent and Trademark Office
Crystal Plaza
2021 Jefferson Davis Highway
Arlington, VA 20231
Telephone (703) 557-3158 (Information)

SCIENTIFIC LIBRARY AT THE PATENT AND TRADEMARK OFFICE

Description: Over 120,000 volumes of scientific and technical books. Information is available on foreign patents. A search room is provided.

Contact: Patent and Trademark Office
Scientific Library
Crystal Plaza
2021 Jefferson Davis Highway
Arlington, VA 20231

OFFICE OF TECHNOLOGY ASSESSMENT AND FORECAST

Description: This office seeks to stimulate the use of the patent files. Each patent represents a new technology and some increment of technological activity. The purpose of the office is to assemble, analyze and make available data, and to identify clear trends in patenting and areas of technology in which there is a high proportion of activity. OTAF produces information in areas of technology with rapid growth. Provides business and government with a single source from which to obtain information covering the entire spectrum of technology. Special areas include: Patents and patent data, technology assessment for technology activities, new technology, energy and energy technology and patent ownership.

Periodically OTAF issues general distribution publications. Of particular interest are Reports Sixth, Seventh and Eighth.

Sixth Report: June 1976 — Reviews 15 technologies with unusually high activity by foreign resident inventors, and 22 high overall activity technologies. Includes information on patent activity in solar and other natural energy sources, and adds reports on the use of waste material and wind for energy generation.

Seventh Report: March 1977 — Reviews historical patenting and trademark registration trends, and includes an extensive collection of historical U.S. patent data. Presents brief reviews of 16 technologies experiencing high overall or foreign patent activity.

Eighth Report: Dec. 1977 — Reviews U.S. patenting in the context of domestic versus international patenting and analyzes the balance of patenting between the U.S. and other countries. Presents a study demonstrating the uniqueness of patents and the patent file as a technological resource. Concludes with an in-depth analysis of patent activity in geophysical exploration, hydrocarbons.

Additionally OTAF prepares specialized reports tailored to individual needs. They assemble, analyze and make available in a number of formats meaningful information about the patent files. In most instances interest will be limited to particular technological areas or to particular patentees. All special reports are prepared on a cost reimbursable basis. These costs may vary from as low as $25.00 to several thousand for complex and large scale treatments of many technological categories requiring extensive time or professional services.

Contact: Office of Technology Assessment and Forecast
Office of Asst. Secretary for Science and Technology
202 Jefferson Davis Highway
Arlington, VA 20231

DISTRICT OFFICES

The Department of Commerce is able to utilize the Department of Commerce, Lockheed Dialog System, Predicasts Data Bases for searches on many subjects for individuals on an hourly basis.

Contact: Boston
441 Stuart Street
Boston, MA 02116

Chicago
55 East Monroe Street
Chicago, IL 60603

Dallas
1100 Commerce Street
Dallas, TX 75242

Detroit
231 West Lafayette Street
Detroit, MI 48226

Greensboro
P.O.Box 1950
Greensboro, NC 27402

Los Angeles
11777 San Vicente Ave.
Los Angeles, CA

Minneapolis
110 South 4th Street
Minneapolis, MN 55401

St. Louis
120 South Central Ave.
St. Louis, MO 63105

NATIONAL BUREAU OF STANDARDS

LIBRARY

Description: Subjects include physical sciences (technical and engineering) mathematics, physics, mechanics, acoustics, optics, spectroscopy, nuclear physics, magnetic properties, chemistry, and chemical analysis.

Library does literature searches both manually and by computer. Acts as referral service for public inquiries within NBS.

Contact: NBS Library
Washington, DC 20234
Telephone (301) 921-3451

NATIONAL STANDARD REFERENCE DATA SYSTEM (NSRDS)

Description: Program management is carried out by the Office of Standard Reference Data. Concerned with data systems and centers, NSRDS has the mission of providing critically evaluated numeric data in a convenient and accessible form to the scientific and technical community. The data centers and special data evaluation projects compile data from the literature and carry out evaluation. NBS administers, aids and subsidizes a publication and data dissemination program which includes a quarterly journal, publications, inquiries, and data information service.

In terms of major applications of the outputs, current projects fall into the following categories.

Energy and Environmental Data — This program includes projects dealing with data that have an important application in some aspect of energy R&D or environmental quality improvement. Projects in chemical kinetics, nuclear properties, spectroscopic data, and interaction of radiation with matter are currently incorporated in this program. The output of these projects is particularly important in R&D on new energy sources, environmental monitoring techniques, and prediction of the effects of pollutants introduced into air, water, or land.

Industrial Process Data — Projects dealing with thermodynamic, transport, colloid and surface, and physical properties of industrially important substances are included in this program. Such data have particular application to design of new processes in the chemical and metallurgical industries, optimization of currently used processes, and general productivity enhancement.

Materials Utilization Data — This program covers properties required for material selection and R&D on new materials. The structural, optical, electric, magnetic and mechanical properties of solid materials are included.

Physical Science Data — Projects which involve basic data of very broad applicability, or which are associated with an important frontier field of science, are included in this program. Examples are fundamental physical constants, data on fundamental particles, and data relevant to radioastronomy.

Contact: NBS
              NSRDS
              Office of Standard Reference Data
              Washington, DC 20234
              Telephone (301) 921-2467

DATA ANALYSIS CENTERS

Alloy Data Center

Description: Collects and evaluates and disseminates phase diagrams, nuclear magnetic resonance and other data dealing with alloy physics. Services available are referral, bibliography compilation, technical analysis and evaluation. These are available to the public for a nominal fee.

Contact: NBS
Alloy Data Center
Center for Materials Science
Washington, DC 20234
Telephone (301) 921-2917

Atomic Collision Cross Section Information Center

Description: Compiles and critically reviews data on collisions between photons, ions, atoms, and molecules of interest to aeronomy, plasma physics, astrophysics, gas discharges and lasers.

Provides referral, bibliography and data compilations, technical analysis and evaluation to the scientific community.

Publishes bibliographies. Available from DDC/NTIS. Other publications available through NTIS and GPO.

Contact: NBS
Atomic Collision Cross Section Information Center
Joint Institute for Laboratory Astrophysics
University of Colorado
Boulder, CO 80309
Telephone (303) 492-7801

Atomic Energy Levels Data Information Center

Description: Collects and evaluates and disseminates information pertaining to atomic spectra and atomic levels for both neutral and ionic species. Also serves as a central reference source for energy level data.

Provides data compilation, state of the art studies, referral, technical analysis and evaluation to all scientific personnel.

Publishes research reports.

Contact: NBS
Atomic Energy Levels Data Information Center
Center for Radiation Research
Washington, DC 20234
Telephone (301) 921-2011

Data Center for Atomic Transitions Probabilities and Atomic Line Shapes and Shifts

Description: Evaluates data on the broadening and shifting of spectral lines of atoms and atomic ions by neutral and ionized gases and plasmas. Collects and disseminates data on radiative transition probabilities of atoms and atomic ions in the gas phase.

Provides technical answers, bibliography and data compilation, literature surveys, referral, and technical analysis and evaluation to the scientific community.

Publishes bibliographies/tables of critically evaluated data.

Contact: NBS
             Data Center for Atomic Transitions Probabilities and Atomic
               Line Shapes and Shifts
             Institute for Basic Standards
             Washington, DC 20234
             Telephone (301) 921-2071

Chemical Kinetics Data Center

Description: Deals with rates of homogeneous, chemical reactions in gas,
              liquid and solid phases.

              Provides bibliography compilation and referral to the scientific
              community.

              Publishes a bibliography on chemical kinetics of chemiexcita-
              tions and energy transfer processes.

Contact: NBS
              Chemical Kinetics Data Center
              Center for Thermodynamics and Molecular Science
              Washington, DC 20234
              Telephone (301) 921-2174

Cryogenic Data Center

Description: Acquires and catalogs for bibliographic purposes all literature
              and data of interest in cryogenics and evaluates and compiles
              low temperature data on properties of materials.

              Provides bibliography compilation, data compilation, literature
              surveys, referral, technical analysis and evaluations.

              Publishes thermodynamic charts, quarterly surveys, biweekly
              announcements and bulletins.

Contact: Cryogenic Data Center
              NBS
              Center for Mechanical Engineering and Process Technology
              Boulder, CO 80302
              Telephone (303) 447-3257

Electrolyte Data Center

Description: Information on electrolytes, electrolytic cells, ionic current,
              voltage, thermodynamic properties, electrodes, transport prop-
              erties, heats of solution and free energy, entropy.

              Provides data compilation, referral and technical analysis and
              evaluation to anyone in electrolytic corrosion and battery elec-
              trowinning industries and to research workers studying chemi-
              cal equilibria in aqueous and nonaqueous solutions, environ-
              mental pollution and energy storage systems.

Contact: NBS
              Electrolyte Data Center
              Center for Thermodynamics and Molecular Science
              Washington, DC 20234
              Telephone (301) 921-3632 extension 2771

Ion Energetics Data Center

Description: Concerned with ionization of atoms, molecules, gas ionizations, ionized gases, energy of gases, molecular properties, atomic properties, ionization potentials.

Provides bibliography and data compilation, indexing, literature surveys, state of the art studies, referral, and technical analysis, evaluation and answers to the public.

Publishes Annotated Bibliography on Proton Affinities.

Contact: NBS
Ion Energetics Data Center
Center for Thermodynamics and Molecular Science
Washington, DC 20234
Telephone (301) 921-2793

Photonuclear Data Center

Description: Concerned with photon reactions, electromagnetic radiation, nuclear cross sections, proton reactions and gamma-neutron reactions, nuclear inelastic scattering, electron scattering and nuclear scattering.

Provides bibliography and data compilation, indexing, literature surveys, state of the art studies, referral, and technical analysis and evaluation to all scientists.

Publishes Data Index and Supplements, and Photonuclear Reaction Data.

Contact- NBS
Photonuclear Data Center
Center for Radiation Research
Washington, DC 20234
Telephone (301) 921-2625

Thermodynamics Research Center

Description: Information on data related to physical, thermodynamic and spectral properties of pure organic compounds and mixtures.

Provides referral, basic research data compilation, literature surveys, technical analysis and evaluation.

Publishes loose leaf data sheets on selected physical and thermodynamic properties and on spectral data of organic compounds and some inorganic compounds and their mixtures.

Contact: Thermodynamics Research Center
Department of Chemistry
Texas A&M University
College Station, TX
Telephone (713) 846-8765

Chemical Thermodynamics Data Center

Description: Provides and maintains self-consistent tables of best values of enthalpy and Gibbs free energy of formation, entropy, heat capacity and phase change properties for chemical compounds.

Provides referral, data compilation, indexing, technical analysis and evaluation, and research reports.

Publishes "Selected Values of Chemical Thermodynamic Properties," "Self-Consistent Tables of Chemical Thermodynamic Properties" and "Annotated Index to Thermodynamic Studies of Inorganic Substances."

Contact: NBS
Center for Thermodynamics and Molecular Science
Washington, DC 20234
Telephone (301) 921-2773

High Pressure Data Center

Description: Reviews, evaluates and disseminates experimental data in the high pressure field. Maintains complete references to all pressure studies from 1 kilobar up to the megabar range.

Provides referral, bibliography and data compilation, indexing, literature surveys and technical analysis and evaluation available to scientific personnel.

Contact: Brigham Young University
High Pressure Data Center
5093 HBLL
Provo, UT
Telephone (801) 374-1211

Superconductive Materials Data Center

Description: Information on superconductive materials. Subject areas include superconductivity, superconductors, magnetic properties, temperature, critical temperature, crystal structure, specific heat, magnetic fields, materials, metals, alloys, thermal properties, carbides, nitrides.

Provides referral, data compilation, technical analysis and evaluation to scientific and technical personnel.

Publishes annual report on new data. Periodic summations of all known data on superconductive materials and materials tested for superconductivity.

Contact: General Electric R&D Center
Schenectady, NY 12301
Telephone (518) 346-8771

X-ray and Ionizing Radiation Data Center

Description: Provides x-ray attenuation data for radiation shielding design analysis of nuclear physics.

Provides referral, data compilation, technical analysis and evaluation. Publishes NBS reports, Scientific Compendia.

Contact: NBS
X-ray and Ionizing Radiation Data Center
Washington, DC 20234
Telephone (301) 921-2685

Crystal Data Center

Description: Identifies crystalline materials by single crystals. Collects and maintains data and information on crystalline materials.

Provides referral data compilation to scientific and technical personnel.

Contact: NBS
Crystal Data Center
Washington, DC 20234
Telephone (301) 921-2950

Diffusion in Metal Data Center

Description: Information on diffusion in metals and their alloys; diffusion coefficients; activation energies for diffusion.

Answers inquiries from government agencies, contractors, research institutions and industry.

Contact: NBS
Diffusion in Metal Data Center
Center for Materials Science
Washington, DC 20234
Telephone (301) 921-3351

Molecular Spectra Data Center

Description: Disseminates data on microwave absorption lines, microwave spectra of molecules and the physical properties derived therefrom. In addition evaluates data on high resolution infrared spectra.

Answers inquiries and provides data compilation to the public.

Information is published in the Journal of Physical Chemical Reference Data.

Contact: NBS
Center for Thermodynamics and Molecular Science
Molecular Spectra Data Center
National Measurement Laboratory
Washington, DC 20234
Telephone (301) 921-2021

Center for Information and Numerical Data Analysis and Synthesis

Description: Maintains a national data base on thermophysical, electronic, electrical, magnetic, and optical properties of materials, and it provides comprehensive and authoritative data analysis services. Searches for, collects, evaluates, analyzes, synthesizes, and condenses the available information and data on selected properties of materials. A major project consists of a "Handbook on the Properties of Rocks and Minerals." Covers the mechanical, physical, electrical, magnetic, and thermophysical properties of rocks and minerals as well as the phenomena of heat flow in the crust of the earth.

Provides data prediction, recommendations and consulting, retrospective searches, document copy procurement and bibliographic searches.

Publishes major books, reports and other publications.

Contact: CINDAS/Purdue University
2595 Yeager Rd.
West Lafayette, IN 47906
Telephone (800) 428-7675 or (317) 463-1581

CENTER FOR BUILDING TECHNOLOGY INFORMATION

Description: Computer-aided document referral system. Assists public and government in locating and obtaining energy-related documents. Contains information on energy conservation in buildings, coal, natural gas, hydropower and nuclear energy.

Contact: NBS
Center for Building Technology Information
Washington, DC 20234
Telephone (301) 921-3377

NATIONAL OCEANIC ATMOSPHERIC ADMINISTRATION

6001 Executive Blvd.
Rockville, MD 20852
Public Affairs (301) 443-8243

Environmental Data and Information Service

Description: Disseminates technical and scientific data for NOAA. Subject areas include environment, climate hydrology, space environments, marine geophysics, atmospheric physics, astrophysics, geophysics.

Provides referral, technical answers, technical analysis and evaluation, abstracting, bibliography and data compilation to the public.

Contact: NOAA
Environmental Data Service
3300 Whitehaven Street NW
Washington, DC 20234
Telephone (202) 343-6454

Environmental Data Index

Description: ENDEX uses environmental files and information. Subjects include aeronomy, environment-related data, engineering, geodesy, hydrology, marine biology, and space solar science.

Provides query capabilities to the public.

Contact: NOAA
Environmental Data and Information Service
Environmental Data Index
3300 Whitehaven St. NW
Washington, DC 20234
Telephone (202) 343-3439

National Geophysical and Solar Terrestrial Data Center

Description: Includes information on solid earth geophysics, solar terrestrial physics.

Provides computer listings, plots, publications, microfilm, photographs, magnetic tapes.

Contact: NOAA
Environmental Data and Information Service
National Geophysical and Solar Terrestrial Data Center
2001 Wisconsin Ave. NW
Washington, DC 20234
Telephone (202) 343-7368

Center for Environmental Assessment

Description: Makes assessments on the impact of critical natural resources: energy, transportation, and marine environment.

Contact: NOAA
Environmental Data and Information Service
Center for Environmental Assessment
3300 Whitehaven Street NW
Washington, DC 20234
Telephone (202) 634-7251

Department of Defense

Pentagon
Washington, DC 20301
Locator (202) 545-6700   Public Affairs (202) 695-9082

LIBRARY AND ANALYSIS CENTERS

DEFENSE NUCLEAR AGENCY TECHNICAL LIBRARY DIVISION

Description: The subject areas include nuclear weapons, weapon effects, radiation effects, explosion effects, electromagnetic pulses, thermal radiation, underground and underwater explosives. Provides RDT&E reports to qualified users of DDC. Unclassified reports available through NTIS. Information available to DNA, DNA contractors and government agencies.

Contact: Defense Nuclear Agency
Technical Library Division
6801 Telegraph Road
Washington, DC 20305
Telephone (202) 325-7780
Ms. Patricia Means

DEFENSE ANALYSIS CENTERS

DOD Nuclear Information and Analysis Center

Description: Information is available that is pertinent to DOD nuclear weapons as it affects research and technology systems (nuclear explosions, radiation and electromagnetic fields). Provides technical analysis and evaluation, data compilation, reference and referral to government agencies and contractors. Publishes technical notes, reports, bibliographies.

52

Contact: DOD Nuclear Information and Analysis Center
GE Tempo
816 State Street
Santa Barbara, CA 93102
Telephone (805) 965-0551
Manager, Warren Chan

Thermophysical and Electric Properties Information Analysis Center

Description: The center is operated by CINDAS at Purdue University. Subject areas include electronic, electrical properties, energy bands, energy gap, energy levels, hall effect, thermophysical properties, thermal conductivity, diffusion, solar radiation, emission ratios, Prandtl number, thermal expansion, specific heat, viscosity.

Provides basic research, consultant data compilation, literature surveys, referral, technical analysis and evaluation to the scientific community.

Publishes data sheets, special reports, retrieval guides to thermophysical properties research literature, and retrieval guides to electronic properties.

Contact: Thermophysical and Electronic Properties Information Ctr.
CINDAS
Purdue University
2595 Yeagoer Rd.
West Lafayette, IN 47906
Telephone (317) 463-1581 or (800) 418-7675

Nondestructive Testing Information Analysis Center

Description: Performs all nondestructive testing and/or evaluation techniques, involving material energy interaction phenomena, e.g., radiography, holography and acoustic magnetics.

Provides referral, reviews, data and bibliography compilations to government agencies and the private sector. Publishes newsletter, technology assessments, and reports.

Contact: Nondestructive Testing Information Analysis Center
Southwest Research Institute
Box 28510
San Antonio, TX 78284
Telephone (512) 684-5111 ext 2361

Chemical Propulsion Information Agency

Description: Technical areas include chemical synthesis: manufacturing process development, thermochemistry; combustion and exhaust plume phenomena: physical, chemical, mechanical, and ballistic properties of propellants and fuels, materials areas specifically related to missile and space propulsion, and overall propulsion unit operational serviceability.

Provides abstracting, indexing, state of the art studies, technical answers, data compilation, directory, compilation, cost analysis and referral to government agencies and contractors.

Publishes abstracts and manuals covering chemical propulsion, newsletters, and state of the art reports.

Contact: Chemical Propulsion Information Agency
Applied Physics Laboratory
John Hopkins University
John Hopkins Rd.
Laurel, MD 20810
Telephone (301) 953-7100, extension 7800
Dr. Peter Nichols

Infrared Information and Analysis Center

Description: Subject areas include infrared research, infrared detection, radiation equipment, thermal cryogenics, solid state physics, infrared radiation, and infrared equipment lasers.

Provides consultant, referral, technical analysis and evaluation to government agencies and contractors. Minimum annual subscription fee for regular users is $230/yr. Publishes IRIS proceedings and IRIA annotated bibliography of infrared literature.

Contact: Infrared Information and Analysis Center
Environmental Research Institute of Michigan
P.O. Box 8618
Ann Arbor, MI 48107
Telephone (313) 994-1200, extension 214

NAVY

LABORATORIES

Naval Research Laboratory, Technical Information Division

Description: Subject areas include chemistry, electricity, metallurgy, nuclear, atomic and optical physics, ocean science engineering, radar, solid state physics. Provides referral, abstracting, identification service, and indexing for visitors upon request. Publishes NRL reports, memorandum reports, monthly progress reports, bibliographies, tests and evaluation reports on specific projects as well as completed research studies.

Contact: Naval Research Laboratory
Technical Information Division
Washington, DC 20375
Telephone (202) 767-2357
E.E. Kirbridge

David W. Taylor Naval Ship R&D Center, Annapolis

Description: RDT/E for areas of shipboard machinery, power systems, electrical systems, automation and control systems, ship silencing, marine propulsion, energy and related fields of science and technology. Provides referral, technical analysis and evaluation to Navy and government personnel. Publications are available through DDC.

Contact: David W. Taylor Naval Ship R&D Center
             Propulsion and Auxiliary Systems Department
             Annapolis, MD 21402
             Telephone (301) 267-2856

Naval Weapons China Lake Technical Information Center

Description: Subject areas include propulsion research, systems and fuels. Provides reference, indexing, and referral to government agencies and contractors. Publishes journals, reports, and materials available through DDC.

Contact: Naval Weapons China Lake Technical Information Center
             China Lake, CA 93555

Weapons Evaluation Facility, Albuquerque

Description: Evaluates and engineers nuclear and assigned nonnuclear weapon systems, nuclear warfare, nuclear explosion, radiation and thermal radiation. Publishes reports on nuclear effects. Available through DDC or a few through NTIS.

Contact: Weapons Evaluation Facility, Albuquerque
             Kirtland AFB
             NM, 87117
             Telephone (505) 264-9805
             J.J. Lahr, Capt. USN

ARMY

ARMY RESEARCH OFFICE

Description: Research supports research in technical areas important to the Army in electronics, mathematics, physical engineering, life and environmental sciences.

             Provides basic research, technical answers, and referral to industry and the general technology community. Publishes books, government reports, scientific and technical data available from DDC.

Contact: Army Research Office
             Research Triangle Park
             Information Processing Office
             P.O. Box 12211
             Research Triangle Park, NC 27709
             Telephone (919) 549-0641

REDSTONE SCIENTIFIC INFORMATION CENTER

Description: Principal data bank for information on the developing and testing of missiles, rockets, propellants, and related items. Contains information on infrared detectors, acoustics, astronautics and energy technology.

Provides referral and technical information to DOD/NASA plus their local contractors with the need to know plus clearance. Publishes technical and scientific data compilations and bibliographies in support of the Army Missile Research and Development and NASA's Marshall Space Flight Center Programs.

Contact: Redstone Scientific Information Center
Redstone Arsenal, AL 35809
Telephone (205) 876-3251

HARRY DIAMOND LABS, SCIENCE AND TECHNICAL INFORMATION OFFICE

Description: Subject areas include ordnance, fuzes, army research, nuclear radiation, nuclear weapons and their effects, electronics, solids, radiation effects, thermodynamics, and operation research. Provides reference, referral, and scientific and technical data to government agencies, universities and government contractors with the need to know. Publishes technical reports, notes on development type material, and technical progress reports available through DDC.

Contact: Harry Diamond Labs, Adelphi MD
Scientific and Technical Information Office
2800 Powder Mill Road
Adelphi, MD 20783
Telephone (202) 394-1010
Chief, John Carrier

ARMY MOBILITY EQUIPMENT RESEARCH AND DEVELOPMENT COMMAND, FT BELVOIR TECHNICAL LIBRARY

Description: Subject areas include electric power sources, fuels, lubricants, electrical and environmental equipment. Provides reference and referral to DOD and contractors. Publishes MERADCOM technical reports.

Contact: MERADCOM
Ft Belvoir Technical Library
Ft Belvoir, VA 22060
Telephone (703) 664-5840

ARMY MATERIEL DEVELOPMENT & READINESS COMMAND, SCIENCE AND TECHNOLOGY DIVISION

Description: Subject areas include radio and radiation chemistry, nuclear warfare, explosives, and liquid and solid propellants. Provides literature searches and periodicals.

Contact:　Army Materiel Development & Readiness Command
Bldg. 59
Attention: DRDAR-TSS
Dover, NJ 07801
Telephone (201) 328-2914

AIR FORCE

AERO PROPULSION LAB, WRIGHT PATTERSON AFB, OHIO

Description:　Formulates research and development programs in aerospace power generation (jet engine fuels, and lubricants). Provides consulting, technical answers, referral, research reports, and scientific and technical data to government agencies. Publishes technical reports available through DDC.

Contact:　Aero Propulsion Lab
Wright Patterson AFB, OH 45433
Telephone (513) 257-1110, extension 53990
W.E. Gardner, Information Officer

AIR FORCE GEOPHYSICS LAB, HANSCOM AFB TECHNICAL LIBRARY

Description:　Subject areas include electronics, geophysics (space, environmental conditions), aeronautics, aircraft, astronomy, atmospherics, astrophysics, energy conversion, geochemistry, electrical properties, and electrons. Includes one of the largest environmental and space sciences reference collections.

Provides referral, bibliography compilation, and on line systems, to DOD agencies and contractors. Publishes books, government reports, periodicals. AFGL publishes technical reports available through DDC.

Contact:　AF Geophysics Lab Technical Library
Hanscom AFB, MA 01731
Telephone (617) 861-4895
Director, Dr. Evano Cunka

AIR FORCE WEAPONS LAB, KIRTLAND AFB TECHNICAL LIBRARY

Description:　Emphasis is on nuclear weapons effects, radiation hazards, nuclear safety, and the application of nuclear devices. Provides reference, referral to Kirtland AFB personnel and to agencies.

Contact: Air Force Weapons Lab
                Kirtland AFB
                Technical Library
                Kirtland, NM 87115
                Telephone (505) 264-7449

OFFICE OF SCIENCE RESEARCH, BOLLING FIELD AFB TECHNICAL LIBRARY

Description: AF research in the areas of continuum mechanics, physics, structural properties, materials, fluid mechanics, solid state sciences, boundary layer, aerodynamics, chemistry, ignition combustion. Emphasis is on engineering, chemistry, mathematics, physics, and information sciences. Provides referral and reference to the scientific community.

Contact: Office of Science Research
                Bolling Field AFB
                Technical Library, Bldg. 410
                Washington, DC 20332
                Telephone (202) 767-4910

OFFICE OF SCIENTIFIC RESEARCH, BOLLING FIELD AFB, DOCUMENTS SECTION

Description: Primary areas include AF research, scientific research, continuum mechanics, boundary layer, aerodynamics, physics, structural properties, materials, fluid mechanics ignition. Contains scientific technical documents produced from AFOSR monitored contracts, and grants emphasizing aeromechanics, energetics, chemical sciences, electronic solid state sciences, life sciences, mathematical and information sciences and physics. Provides materials identification, referral and reference. Publishes Proposer's guide to AFOSR research programs.

Contact: Office of Scientific Research
                Bolling Field AFB,
                Documents Section
                Bldg. 410
                Washington, DC 20332
                Telephone (202) 767-4912

TRI SERVICE INDUSTRY INFORMATION CENTER

NAVY ACQUISITION RESEARCH AND DEVELOPMENT CENTER

Description: NARDIC is a focal point for making R&D planning and requirements available to industry. Documents available for review are Science and Technology objectives, Operational Requirements, Advanced Development Objectives, Research and Development Summaries, Research and Technology Work Unit Summaries, Laboratory Program Summaries, and Proceedings of Advanced Planning Briefings for Industry.

Available to industry and organizations that have demonstrated capabilities of engaging or participating in the Navy Industry Cooperative R&D program, or technology transfer programs, or have been registered for access to DOD information service by a DOD component, based on current DOD contract or participation in the potential contractors program of the Army or Air Force.

Contact: Headquarters U.S. Army Material Development and Readiness Command
NARDIC
Room 8S56
5001 Eisenhower Avenue
Alexandria, VA 22333
Telephone (202) 274-9315
Ms. Lillian Morris

ARMY RESEARCH, DEVELOPMENT AND PLANNING INFORMATION FOR INDUSTRY

Description: Provides R&D information on plans and programs. Personnel is available to provide technical consultation and guidance on current and long range research and development projects.

Available to organizations that have the desire to participate in the R&D effort of the Army. Must be able to provide evidence of an existing or planned R&D capability. Must have personnel and facility security clearance.

Contact: HQ DARCOM Tri Service Alexandria
Attention: DRCDE-LO
5001 Eisenhower Avenue
Alexandria, VA 22333
Telephone (202) 274-8948
Ms. Rebekah Liller

AIR FORCE INFORMATION FOR INDUSTRY OFFICE

Description: Air Force makes available the latest planning information. The documents that are available include: General Operational Requirements, Program Management Directives, Planning Conspectus, Technology Needs, Technology Objects, Research Planning Guides, Program Elements, Descriptive Summaries, and Work Unit Information.

Available to organizations that register for access to DOD information services by a DOD component based on a current

DOD contract or are participating in the potential contractor program by the Air Force, Army or Navy.

Contact: Air Force Information for Industry Office
DRCDE-LO
5001 Eisenhower Avenue
Alexandria, VA 22333

Midwest Information for Industry Office
AFAL/TSR
Wright Patterson AFB, OH 45433
Telephone (513) 255-6731

Air Force Information for Industry Office
TSgt Whitaker
1030 East Green Street
Pasadena, CA 91106
Telephone (213) 792-5182

DEFENSE DOCUMENTATION CENTER

Cameron Station
Alexandria, VA 22314
Reference Section (202) 274-7633

DDC is the clearinghouse for DOD collection of R&D in all fields of science and technology. Contains information as related to research, development, test and evaluation. Contains information on what research is planned, performed and the completed results. Department of Defense and associated contract researchers deposit information into data banks collected by DDC.

DATA BANKS

(1)   R&DPP—repository of program planning documentation at the project and task level.

(2)   R&T Work Unit Information System—Collection of technically oriented summaries describing research and technical projects currently in progress at the work unit level. Information is available concerning what, where, when, how, at what costs, by whom, and under whose sponsorship research is performed.

(3)   Technical Report Data Bank—Collection of formally documented science and technical results of Department of Defense sponsored research, development, test and evaluation. Products, programs and services are available from the technical report collection in bibliographies, and tape distribution.

(4)   Independent R&D Data Bank—Data bank of information describing the technical progress being performed by DOD contractors as part of their independent R&D programs.

Categories of DDC Data Banks

Aeronautics
Agriculture
Astronomy
Astrophysics
Atmospheric Sciences
Behavioral and Social Sciences
Biological and Medical Sciences
Chemistry
Earth Sciences and Oceanography
Electrical Engineering
Energy Conversion (Nonpropulsive) Materials
Mathematical Sciences
Engineering
Military Sciences
Missile Technology
Navigation
Nuclear Science and Technology
Ordnance
Physics
Properties and Fuels
Space Technology

By-Products of the Data Banks

(A)   Announcement publications

(B)   Automatic document tape—microfiche copies

(C)   Automatic magnetic tape distribution program (includes all DDC R&D reports during a two week period)

(D)   Bibliographies (progress listings of technical reports related to special subjects)

(E)   Defense R&D of the 1960s

(F)   Defense R&D of the 1970s

(G)   Selective dissemination of information (7-project package of any of DDC's tape products)

(H)   Technical vocabulary

(I)   Recurring management information systems reports

OTHER SERVICES OFFERED

(A)   DDC Referral Service—data bank of government sponsored activities specializing in scientific and technical information not available in DDC

(B)   Central Registry—central file of users with authorized access to DOD science and technology information

(C)   DOD RDT&E on-Line System—network of remote terminal stations linked to DDC central computer for instant visual display of data from 4 major collections

ANNOUNCEMENTS OF DDC PROGRAMS, PRODUCTS AND SERVICES

(A)   Technical Abstract Bulletin
(B)   Technical Abstract Bulletin Index
(C)   Annual Indexes
(D)   TAB Quarterly Indexes
(E)   Bibliography of Bibliographies

ELIGIBILITY REQUIREMENTS

Individuals that have R&D activities within the Federal government and their associated contractors, subcontractors and grantees with current contracts may be eligible for service by military service authorization under DOD potential contractor project.

REGISTRATION

Registration for DDC services assists the user in obtaining services offered by Defense sponsored Information Analysis Centers and major technical libraries.

Registration Procedures

(1)   Requester will be sent manual entitled *Registration for Science and Technical Information Services of Defense.* This manual explains the procedures.

(2)   Requester will recieve a DOD user Code number and be placed on a central registry.

(3)   Requester will receive a duplicate copy of DD form 1540 with appropriate materials.

ORDERING PUBLICATIONS

Two options are open to individuals: (1) Order directly through NTIS with check, money order or with an American Express Card number. (2) Order directly from DDC or NTIS after establishment of a NTIS Deposit Account. DDC users are encouraged to open an NTIS Deposit Account since faster service can be provided.

CLASSIFIED INFORMATION

Requesters that require classified services are required to complete DD form 1541. If certified to receive classified services, complete DDC form to receive copies of Technical Abstract Bulletin.

Contact for Forms DD 1540 and DD 1541:   DDC-TSR
                                            202-274-6871
                                            IDS 107-46872
                                            Autovon 28-46872

Contact for Service Information:	DDC-TSR-1 202 274-7633, 34, or 35 IDS 107-47633, 34, 35 Autovon 28-47633, 34, 35
24 Hour Document Ordering Service:	202-274-6811
24 Hour WVIS Service:	202-274-6996
Office of Science and Technology:	202-274-6980
Office of Public Affairs:	202-274-6881
For Initial Information Contact:	DDC Attention: DDC-TSR Alexandria, VA 22314 202-274-7633, 34, 35 IDS 107-47633, 34,35 Autovon 28-47633, 34, 35

HOW DDC SERVES THE GENERAL PUBLIC

Unidentified Requests

DDC responds to letters from industry, research and educational institutions, and state and local governments, asking for information on the availability of technical reports. Searches of DDC collection are performed and the requester is advised if the report is available and how and from what source copies may be obtained.

If a DOD sponsored report is not available to the public, DDC will forward a request to the military controlling office to determine if the existing limitation may be waived. If DDC receives authority for public release, the report is released to all requesters through NTIS. If selective release to the individual requester is approved, a copy will be furnished by DDC subject to the conditions placed on its release. If the release is disapproved, the military controlling office notifies the requester.

If the report cannot be identified as a DOD sponsored or cosponsored research project, the DDC representative contacts other government and nongovernment organizations to locate and determine availability, cost and other pertinent data.

SERVICE TO LEGAL PROFESSION

Attorneys that are in search for substantiating evidence regarding proposed or anticipated litigation can contact DDC to request information concerning announcements of specific reports to the general public and disposition of patent ownerships resulting from particular research projects sponsored or cosponsored by the Defense Department.

UNCLASSIFIED/UNLIMITED DOD REPORTS

DDC provides copies of those R&D reports sponsored or generated by the Department of Defense. Additionally reports that were formerly classified or limited are furnished as soon as they are declassified and delimited. NTIS then announces the Defense reports in the publication *Government Reports Announcements and Indexes.*

SERVICE CONTINUED BETWEEN CONTRACTS

Potential Defense Contractors Program

This enables companies, educational institutions, nonprofit technical organizations and separate individuals with adequate R&D capabilities to participate in future development of new systems, improvements to current systems. Any individual or organization whose contract with the Department of Defense has expired may be considered a potential contractor and be eligible.

Registrants will be provided with advance notices annually of long range science and technology objectives and R&D requirements. Special group conferences are held for the purpose of informing registrants of current and proposed programs. Registrants also qualify for access to the scientific and technical data banks at DDC. Access is limited to certified subject categories related to a registrants specific fields of interest.

HOW TO FIND INFORMATION ON THE POTENTIAL DEFENSE CONTRACTORS PROGRAM

DDC performs central registration functions for DOD organizations sponsoring potential Defense contractors programs. Military departments and DARPA execute their own agreements.

        Contact: Department of Army
                        DARCOM
                        5001 Eisenhower Avenue
                        Alexandria, VA 22333
                        Telephone (202) 274-9816

                        Department of Navy
                        Naval Material Command
                        Washington, DC 20360
                        Telephone (202) 692-3004

                        Department of the Air Force
                        Andrews AFB
                        Washington, DC 20334
                        Telephone (301) 981-4632

                        DARPA
                        1400 Wilson Boulevard
                        Arlington, VA 22209
                        Telephone (202) 694-5919

Department of Housing and Urban Development

451 7th Street SW
Washington, DC 20410
Locator (202) 755-5111   Public Affairs (202) 755-5244

INFORMATION SOURCES AND SYSTEMS

NATIONAL SOLAR HEATING AND COOLING INFORMATION CENTER

Description: Established by HUD in cooperation with DOE. Sponsors solar demonstration projects establishing and developing building and performance cost data. Provides information on domestic and foreign technological and nontechnological information on solar heating and cooling.

Contact: HUD
National Solar Heating and Cooling Information Center
Rockville, MD 20850
Telephone (800) 523-2929

NATIONAL SOLAR HEATING AND COOLING SOLAR DOCUMENTATION CENTER

Description: Services the NSHCIC with information on solar heating and cooling of buildings.

Contact: Franklin Institute Research Laboratory
20 and Cherry Street
Philadelphia, PA 19103
Telephone (215) 448-1539

Department of Interior

C Street Between 18th and 19th NW
Washington, DC 20240
Locator (202) 343-1100   Public Affairs (202) 343-3171

U.S. GEOLOGICAL SURVEY

ENERGY RESOURCES DATA SYSTEMS

Coal Data System

Description: Information on the distribution and quality of coal resources, pertinent geologic, geochemical, geophysical petrologic, engineering mining, drill-hole geodetic resource and production data Available through U.S. Geological Survey, Reston VA.

Geotherm

Description: Studies the cyclic behavior of geothermal pools which is reflected in the engineering characteristics. Available from U.S. Geological Survey, Reston VA.

Well History Control System

Description: Basic categories of data related to the drilling and compilation of oil and gas wells: (1) location, (2) initial potential, (3) formulation, (4) cores and (5) brillstem tests and miscellaneous drilling data. Available from a file purchased from and maintained by Petroleum Information Corporation (Denver).

Petroleum Data Systems

Description: Provides production and reservoir data to conduct resource estimates of remaining petroleum. Data covers geology engineering and production. Available through University of Oklahoma. Available in GE Mark III worldwide sharing network.

Oil Shale Data Bank

Description: Information derived from existing drill cores. Contains geochemical, geological data on all shale occurrences. Available
through U.S. Geological Survey, Denver Colorado.

CRIB MINERAL RESOURCES

Description: Data bank of U.S. Geological Survey. Contains information on
metallic and nonmetallic mineral resources. File is orientated
toward mineral deposits and commodities. Information consists of descriptive text, numeric data codes and certain key
words. Approximately 300 data items are available.

Available to public through computer facilities at University of
Oklahoma and GE.

Contact: USGS
Office of Public Inquiries
National Center
Reston, VA 22092

Director Information Systems Programs
University of Oklahoma
1808 Newton Drive
Newton, OK 73069

GE
Information Services
Business Division
Rockville, MD 20852

INFORMATION ANALYSIS CENTERS AND SYSTEMS

National Center for Thermodynamic Data of Minerals

Description: Information analysis center of USGS and NBS. Searches the
world literature for thermodynamic properties, minerals, syn-
thetic materials, analogs, geology, materials, temperature, pressure, composition thermodynamics, solid phases, chemical reactions, and gases.

Provides data compilation, technical analysis and evaluation,
abstracting, state of the art reviews, and information retrieval
to the scientific and industrial community. Charges for special
requests. Publishes data tables and evaluation reviews on thermodynamic data.

Contact: USGS
National Center for Thermodynamic Data of Minerals
National Center
Reston, VA 22092

Information Systems, Mineral and Material R&D

Description: Information on the advances in technology used to obtain materials. Publishes R&D reports, bulletins, handbooks, reports, and annual reports

Contact: Department of Interior
U.S. Bureau of Mines
Mineral and Materials R&D
2401 E Street NW
Washington, DC 20241

Mining Research

Description: Aimed at producing technology that will meet energy demands at lowest costs. Includes three categories: (a) mining health and safety, (b) advanced mining techniques and (c) research and resource conservation and environment. Information comes out of 5 research centers Carbondale IL, Denver CO, Minneapolis MN, Pittsburgh PA, Spokane WA.

Publishes bulletins, tech progress reports, report of investigator, open file reports, information circulars and patents.

Contact: Department of Interior
Mining Research
2401 E Street NW
Washington, DC 20241

Helium Division Natural Gases Data Base

Description: Information on gas samples obtained from pipelines and wells.

Contact: Department of Interior
U.S. Bureau of Mines
Helium Division
National Gases Data Base
Box H 4372
Amarillo, TX 79101
Telephone (806) 376-2617

Mineral and Materials Supply/Demand Analysis System

Description: Information on the international supply and demand for minerals and fuels. Provides data collection and analyses to the public. Publishes data bases, surveys, hardbooks, and monthly publications.

Contact: Department of Interior
U.S. Bureau of Mines
Mineral and Materials Supply/Demand Analysis System
2401 E Street NW
Washington, DC 20241

OCS Reference Center

Description: Information on oil and gas activities pertaining to the outer continental shelf. A network will be established in the Department of Interior and other agencies and programs that relate to continental shelf oil and gas issues.

Contact: OCS Referral Center
                Office of OCS Program Coordination
                Department of Interior
                Washington, DC 20240
                Telephone (202) 343-9314

Department of Transportation

400 7th Street SW
Washington, DC 20590
Locator (202) 426-4000

LIBRARY

The library has a comprehensive collection of material for all modes of transportation. Subject areas include highway bridges, engineering, general transportation, traffic engineering, urban transportation, railroads, marine engineering, navigation, law transportation, planning, statistics and all facets of transportation technology.

Contact: Department of Transportation TAD-49
Room 2200
DOT HQ Building
400 7th Street SW
Washington, DC 20590

INFORMATION SYSTEMS, TRISNET

Trisnet links the nation's transportation activities into a system of libraries, data bases and retrieval services. Data is provided by the Highway Research Information Service, Maritime Transportation Research Board, Federal Aviation Administration, Urban Mass Transit Administration, DOT Transportation Systems Center, and DOT Office of International Transportation Systems.

Contact: For information on Trisnet Services
Department of Transportation
Research and Special Programs
 Information Management Branch
400 7th Street SW
Washington, DC 20590
Telephone (202) 426-0975

70

CORE SERVICES

Switching/Referral

Indexing/Abstracting

HRIS—Highway Research Information Service

Contact: HRIS, Manager
             Transportation Research Board
             2101 Constitution Avenue NW
             Washington, DC 20418
             Telephone (202) 389-6358

RRIS—Railroad Research Information Service

Contact: RRIS, Manager
             Transportation Research Board
             2101 Constitution Avenue NW
             Washington, DC 20418
             Telephone (202) 389-6611

MRIS—Maritime Research Information Service

Contact: MRIS
             Transportation Research Board
             2101 Constitution Avenue NW
             Washington, DC 20418
             Telephone (202) 389-6687

ATRIS—Air Transport Research Information Service

Contact: ATRIS
             Transportation Research Board
             2101 Constitution Avenue NW
             Washington, DC 20418
             Telephone (202) 389-6611

HSL—Highway Safety Literature Service

Contact: NHTSA
             Technical Reference Division
             NASSIF Building
             Room 5108
             400 7th Street SW
             Washington, DC 20590
             Telephone (202) 426-2987

TRIC—Transit Research Information Center

Contact: Urban Mass Transit Administration
             TRIC
             Technical Information Specialist
             2100 2nd Street SW
             Washington, DC 20590
             Telephone (202) 426-9157

Tris On-Line Service

This is a computerized information retrieval system of selected reference technical literature and on-going research resumes accessible from computer terminals via telephone lines.

Subjects include analytical technology, construction methods, safety, economics, energy, environmental effects, social effects.

Information types include abstracts of technical reports and articles, directories to data collections, directories to information services, numerical tables and data base, planning/policy studies, R&D on-going project resumes and rules/regulations.

Transportation modes include air, highway, pipeline, rail and water transport. Tris On-Line may be used from individual companies or organization terminals. All Trisnet services have such terminals, and for the cost of the search, will assist with information requirements.

    Contact: DOT/TSC
                U.S. Department of Transportation
                Cambridge, MA 02142
                Telephone (617) 494-2486

Document Delivery Services

    Contact: Library Director, DOT/LIB
                U.S. Department of Transportation
                400 Seventh Street SW
                Washington, DC 20590
                Telephone (202) 426-2565

                Librarian, ITS/LIB Berkeley
                Institute of Transportation Studies
                412 McLaughlin Hall
                University of California
                Berkeley, CA 94720
                Telephone (415) 642-3604

                DOT/TIC
                Head Information Services Branch
                Kendall Square
                Cambridge, MA 02142
                Telephone (617) 494-2016

                Librarian, NUTC/LIB
                Northwestern University Transportation Center Library
                Evanston, IL 60201
                Telephone (312) 492-5273

                DOT Technical Documentation Center
                c/o NTIS
                5285 Port Royal Road
                Springfield, VA 22161
                Telephone (703) 451-4468

SECTION II
ADMINISTRATIVE AGENCIES

Environmental Protection Agency

401 M Street, SW
Washington, DC 20460
Locator (202) 755-2673
Public Affairs (202) 755-0700

LIBRARY

Information on pollution control from energy sources. Contains computerized bibliographic sources. Emphasis is on water pollution.

Contact: Library
EPA
401 M Street, SW
Washington, DC 20506
Telephone (202) 755-0308

INFORMATION SOURCES AND SYSTEMS

OFFICE OF AIR QUALITY PLANNING AND STANDARDS

National Emissions Data System

Description: Centralized data bank that contains engineering data on air pollution in the U.S. The system is used to identify and locate emitting sources. Publishes NEDS data base; can be used to obtain reports and listings for the public.

Contact: EPA
Office of Air Quality Planning and Standards
National Emissions Data System
Research Triangle Park, NC 27711
Telephone (919) 629-5201

Energy Data System

Description: Centralized file that provides management with a flexible energy environmental data base for evaluating problems associated with stationary source, fuel usage, fuel quality, compliance with emission regulations, and related effects on air quality

Publishes reports that contain a wide range of energy information and cover such specific areas as fuel use.

Summaries by geographical region and by fuel-consuming categories, emission and equipment installed at large fuel-burning sources, regulations applicable to large fuel-burning sources, compliance schedules and status modeling results for large powerplants and air quality data in the vicinity of large powerplants.

Contact: EPA
Office of Air Quality Planning and Standards
Research Triangle Park, NC 27711
Telephone (919) 629-5201

ENVIRONMENTAL MONITORING AND SUPPORT LABORATORY

Description: Collection of information on nuclear science broadened to include all aspects of environmental science. Provides computerized literature searches, reference services.

Contact: EPA
Environmental Monitoring and Support Laboratory
PO Box 15027
Las Vegas, NV 89114
Telephone (702) 736-2969

AIR POLLUTION TECHNICAL INFORMATION CENTER

Description: Information on pollution measurements, effects and control. Provides bibliographies, retrieval services and referral services. Publishes *Air Pollution Abstracts*.

Contact: EPA
Air Pollution Technical Information Center
Research Triangle Park, NC 27711
Telephone (919) 549-8411

SOLID WASTE INFORMATION RETRIEVAL SYSTEM

Description: SWIRS is a bibliographic system which provides access to international literature in solid waste information. Provides literature searches, retrieval services, referrals to the public. Publishes abstracts and publications.

Contact: SWIRS
                1835 K Street, NW
                Washington, DC 20460
                Telephone (202) 254-6434

General Services Administration

General Services Building
18th and F Streets, NW
Washington, DC 20405
Locator (202) 655-4000
Public Affairs (202) 566-1231
Federal Information Center (202) 755-8660

DATA BANK ON U.S. RESOURCES

Data includes information on physical resources in the U.S. Limited services and inquiries. Publishes *Resource Data Catalog.*

Contact: Federal Preparedness Agency
18th and F Street, NW
Washington, DC 20405
Telephone (202) 343-8514

NASA

400 Maryland Avenue, SW
Washington, DC 20546
Headquarters Information (202) 755-2320

LIBRARY

LIBRARY NETWORK (NALNET)

Description: NALNET is a cooperative effort between NASA Headquarters and the libraries in the research centers to achieve centralized indexing cataloging and computer processing. The network offers direct on-line access for search and identification to a computerized data base.

Subjects include aeronautics, space research, earth resources, energy and NASA research and development. *New Books* is an informal biweekly notification for NASA scientists, engineers and managers. Data is for NASA libraries.

Contact: Science and Technology Information Office
400 Maryland Avenue, SW
Washington, DC 20546
Telephone (202) 755-3548

INFORMATIONAL SOURCES AND SYSTEMS

RESEARCH AND TECHNOLOGY OBJECTIVES AND PLANS SUMMARY

Description: This document lists supporting research and technology currently in process at NASA. Contains abstracts from approved research and technology objectives and plans.

Contact: NTIS
                5285 Port Royal Road
                Springfield, VA 22161

NASA SCIENTIFIC AND TECHNICAL INFORMATION SYSTEM

Description: The system supports the NASA R&D efforts and assists in the
                dissemination of NASA program generated information to the
                public. The system covers all the sciences and technologies re-
                lated to aeronautics, space-earth resource surveys, solar and
                wind energy and other areas of NASA R&D. Also received are
                aerospace related publications issued by DOD, FAA, DOE,
                EPA, NOAA, NSF and NTIS.

Scientific and Technical Aerospace Reports (STAR)

Description: Subjects include science and technology as related to space.
                STAR announces reports, doctoral theses, NASA patents and
                includes current research projects.

                Publications from internal sources issued through STAR in-
                clude Contractors Reports, Technical Memoranda, and Tech-
                nical Notes and Reports.

Contact: Superintendent of Documents
                Washington, DC 20402

NASA/SCAN

Description: Covers announcements of selected STAR and IAA citations in
                over 200 subject topics available to NASA and contractors.

Contact: Scientific and Technology Information Office
                400 Maryland Avenue, SW
                Washington, DC 20546
                Telephone (202) 755-3548

RECON

Description: Computerized on-line CRT display interactive system for infor-
                mation retrieval from the system data base. Available primarily
                to libraries. The NASA Combined Index is a microfilmed com-
                prehensive index to all the documents in the data base and is
                used by NASA libraries.

                Printed literature searches are made for NASA, NASA contrac-
                tors, universities, and other government agencies and NASA In-
                dustrial Application Centers.

Contact: For copies of NASA publications and microfiche:
                NTIS
                5285 Port Royal Road
                Springfield, VA 22161

AIAA TECHNOLOGY INFORMATION SERVICE

Description: AIAA-TIS is under NASA contract. It acquires worldwide aerospace literature in the form of journal articles, conference papers and books. IAA reproduces the accessioned items and provides a public sales agency for copies of announced publications and submits computer readable cataloging data into NASA's Science and Technology Information System. Available from AIAA is the publication *International Aerospace Abstracts.*

Contact: Technical Information Services
              AIAA
              750 Third Avenue
              New York, NY 10017

PERIODIC BIBLIOGRAPHIES

Description: Subject areas include aeronautical engineering, aerospace medicine and biology, computer program abstracts, earth resources, energy, management, NASA patent abstracts and high energy propellants.

Contact: Science and Technology Information Office
              400 Maryland Avenue, SW
              Washington, DC 20546
              Telephone (202) 755-3548

OFFICE OF TECHNOLOGY UTILIZATION

Description: Each NASA Center has a Technology Utilization Officer (TUO). NASA's Office of Technology Utilization publishes *Tech Briefs.* This publication describes potential products, industrial processes, basic and applied research, computer software, and new sources of technical data. For many of the innovations described in *Tech Briefs*, the center TUO has prepared additional material that will help in detailed evaluation and actual use or construction of new technology.

              The TUO at each center also has other special publications, sponsors conferences, and arranges for expert assistance in solving technical problems.

Contact: Technology Utilization Officer at the closest NASA
                Center or:
              Louis Mogavero
              Technology Utilization Branch
              CODE ETU-6
              NASA Headquarters
              Washington, DC 20546
              Telephone (202) 755-2220

INDUSTRIAL APPLICATION CENTERS

Description: Maintains computerized access to space related reports and reports from nonspace governmental sources. The network has access to 7.5 million documents worldwide.

Major information sources now include: Air Pollution Technical Information Center; Chemical Abstracts Condensates; Engineering Index; Government Reports Announcements; NASA International Aerospace Abstracts; NASA *Tech Briefs*; NASA Scientific and Technical Aerospace Reports; Nuclear Science Abstracts; Selected Water Resources Abstracts; and Educational Resources Information Center.

In addition to these files, IAC utilized specialized files dealing with food technology, textiles technology, metallurgy, medicine, business, economics, and other social and physical sciences.

Basically the applications centers offer three services: (1) retrospective searches (pertinent technical literature that has already been published and filed somewhere is retrieved); (2) current awareness services (consists of abstracts relating to a specific topic tailored to meet exact needs; and (3) technical assistance (applications engineers determine problems and apply solutions from such sources as companies, government agencies, universities and research organizations).

Contact: Knowledge Availability Systems Center
University of Pittsburgh
Pittsburgh, PA 15260
Telephone (412) 624-5211

New England Research Application Center
Mansfield Professional Park
Storrs, CT 06268
Telephone (203) 486-4533

North Carolina Science & Technology Research Center
PO Box 12235
Research Triangle Park, NC 27709
Telephone (919) 549-0671

Technology Application Center
University of New Mexico
Albuquerque, NM 87131
Telephone (505) 277-4000

Western Research Application Center
Room 205
901 Exposition Boulevard
University of Southern California
University Park
Los Angeles, CA 90007
Telephone (213) 741-6132

Aerospace Research Application Center
Indiana University-Purdue University at Indianapolis
1201 East 38th Street
Indianapolis, IN 46205
Telephone (317) 264-4644

NATIONAL SPACE SCIENCE DATA CENTER

Description: Further the latest practicable use of reduced data from or related to space science experiments, NSSDC collects, organizes,
stores, announces, retrieves, disseminates and exchanges data
and information received from experiments. Data is collected
in the fields of astronomy, geodesy and gravimetry, ionospheric
physics, meteorology, particles and field, planetary atmos-
pheres, planetology and solar physics.

Available to scientific and educational users. Publishes reports,
handbooks and *SPACEWARN* Bulletin. Reports are available
through the center and through NTIS.

Contact: NSSDC
NASA/Goddard Space Flight Center
Greenbelt, MD 20771
Telephone (301) 982-2354

COSMIC

Description: Sponsored by NASA to give access to computer programs developed by NASA and DOD and selected programs from other
government agencies. Includes 1,600 computer programs. Subjects range from structural mechanics and thermodynamics to
Information Retrieval and Project Management.

Of particular interest to the scientific community is NASA's
Energy Cost Analysis Program. NECAP was developed as a
computer system used to determine and minimize building energy consumption.

Contact: COSMIC
Suite 112
Barrow Hall
University of Georgia
Athens, GA 30602
Telephone (404) 542-3265

NASA PATENT INFORMATION

Description: Over 3,500 NASA inventions are available for licensing in the
U.S. There are three types of patents: (1) Nonexclusive licenses;
they must be used by a negotiated targeted date, but are usually royalty free. (2) Exclusive; these are granted to encourage

early commercial development by NASA inventions (generally 5 to 10 years) and usually require royalties based on sales or use. (3) NASA-offered foreign patents.

Contact: NTIS
             NASA Patent Abstract Bibliography
             5285 Port Royal Road
             Springfield, VA 22161

National Science Foundation

1800 G Street, NW
Washington, DC 20550
Locator (202) 655-4000
Public Information Branch (202) 632-5722

APPLIED SCIENCE AND RESEARCH APPLICATIONS

ASRA identifies and analyzes major problems with significant scientific and technical content. ASRA also supports areas of basic research that have special relevance to national problems and provides support for research proposals that do not fit within other NSF programs, programs of other agencies or the private sector. ASRA funds research underlying new or developing technologies. Subjects include environment, energy, intergovernmental science and R&D incentives, productivity, expert research and technology assessment.

ASRA publishes this information in various reports and publications. Information is available in the publication *Recent Research Reports.*

Contact: ASRA Information Resources Center
             NSF
             1800 G Street, NW
             Washington, DC 20550
             Telephone (202) 634-4062
             Carmeen Adams

             Documents may be ordered from NTIS

             Department of Commerce
             5285 Port Royal Road
             Springfield, VA 22161

DIRECTORATE FOR SCIENTIFIC TECHNOLOGICAL AND INTERNATIONAL AFFAIRS

DIVISION OF POLICY RESEARCH AND ANALYSIS

Description: Provides information on science and technology policy matters; appraises effectiveness of on-going Federal and National R&D efforts; appraises impact of R&D upon industrial development.

The Division supports analysis programs such as (1) the environment policy research and analysis program, assessing the most effective ways of developing long-term knowledge base for the analysis of energy and environmental protection; and (2) the energy policy studies program, which provides policy analysis contributing to the national energy policy; such policy studies as choices in R&D support for traditional and advanced energy systems, economic aspects of energy policy, the relation of science and technology to renewable and nonrenewable energy resources and environmental issues related to energy systems and energy policy.

SCIENCE RESOURCES STUDIES

Description: Collects statistical data and analyzes resource information including studies of the factors that affect and limit the supply and utilization of science resources. Particular emphasis is given to analyzing and disseminating information on the characteristics and patterns of funding for R&D and other scientific activities of government, industry, universities and nonprofit institutions. Publications include:

A. Full reports

(1) Annual report—an analysis of Federal R&D funding by function
(2) Annual report—R&D in industry
(3) Annual report—national patterns of R&D resources: funds and manpower in U.S.
(4) Annual report—Federal funds for research development and other scientific activities
(5) 1985 R&D funding projections
(6) R&D activities of independent nonprofit institutions
(7) Summary of active awards and completed projects

B. Detailed statistical tables published in advance of full report

(1) Federal funds for research development and other scientific activities

C. Reviews of data on science resources

(1) Reviews of data on science resources, No. 29 "Current and Future Utilization of Scientific and Technical Personnel in Energy Related Activities"

      (2) Reviews of data on science resources, No. 26
"Energy and Energy Related R&D Activities of
Federal Installations and Federally Funded R&D
Centers"

  D. Science resources studies highlights

    (1) Federal R&D funding shows a strong recent rise
but little growth in 1978

    (2) Defense and energy spur Federal R&D growth
FY 1974 to FY 1978

    (3) R&D spending reaches nearly $41 billion in 1977

Nuclear Regulatory Commission

1717 H Street, NW
Washington, DC 20555
Locator (301) 492-7000
Office of Information (301) 492-7715

NUCLEAR REGULATORY COMMISSION LIBRARY

Emphasis is on nuclear reactors, radiological water and air pollution. The library provides reference and referral services.

Contact: Nuclear Regulatory Commission Library
7920 Norfolk Avenue
Bethesda, MD 20014
Mailing address Washington, DC 20555
Telephone (301) 492-7748

SECTION III
QUASI-GOVERNMENT AGENCIES

Smithsonian Science
Information Exchange

1730 M Street
Washington, DC 20036
Locator (202) 381-4211   Information (202) 381-5855

Provides a central place for data on scientific research projects reported by government agencies and other sources organizing major research projects.

SEARCH SERVICES AVAILABLE

Custom Search Service — Search data base for Notices of Research Projects on specific subjects.

Research Information Packages — Information on project notices of high interest.

Selective Dissemination of Information — The exchange offers 2 selective dissemination services in order for individuals or organizations to receive regular updates of custom searches or research information packages.

Custom SDI Service — Provides updates of searches that require scientific review.

Standard SDI Service — Provides updates of research information packages or custom searches that do not require review by scientific staff.

Investigator Searches — Administrative searches are available for all notices of research projects on SSIE's file registered under name of investigator.

Accession Number Searches — Current files may be searched by organization, supporting organization, grant or contract number.

SSIE Science Newsletter — Published 10 times a year.

Custom Searches of the Historical Files — Searches can be made of most recent five years.

Catalogs of Ongoing Research — A series of computer programs produce camera ready copy for catalogs or directories of ongoing research.

Interchange Tapes — Magnetic tapes of segments of the data bases.

Contact: Smithsonian Science Information Exchange
1730 M Street NW
Washington, DC 20036
Telephone (202) 381-5511

SSIE ON-LINE SEARCH SERVICE

Description: Searches prepublication information on research in progress. The exchange collects, indexes, stores and disseminates information about basic and applied research in all fields of the life and physical sciences and interdisciplinary fields such as energy, environmental sciences and urban affairs. The active file covers research either in progress or initiated and completed during the two most recent government fiscal years.

Project descriptions are from organizations that fund research. This can be federal, state and local government agencies, nonprofit associations, foundations, colleges and universities. To a more limited extent private industry and foreign research organizations. Approximately 80% of the information is provided by the agencies of the federal government. This includes data about grants and contracts awarded to outside organizations as well as work carried out in government research centers.

Major subject categories include agricultural sciences, behavioral sciences, chemistry and chemical engineering, earth sciences, electronics and electrical engineering, engineering sciences, materials, mathematics, medical sciences, physics, social sciences and economics.

The basic record in the SSIE system is the single page Notice of Research Project. The information supplied usually includes project title, supporting organization name and project number, performing organization name and project number, name of technical summary of work to be performed.

SSIE users can either request searches conducted by SSIE staff or a search can be made through SDC's search service or through Lockheed's DIALOG Information Retrieval Service.

Contact: SDC Search Service
2500 Colorado Ave.
Santa Monica, CA 90406
Telephone (213) 829-7511

7929 Westpark Drive
McLean, VA 22101
Telephone (703) 790-9850

401 Hackensack Ave.
Hackensack, NJ 07601
Telephone (201) 487-0571

SSIE
Room 300
1730 M Street NW
Washington, DC 20036
Telephone (202) 381-5511

Lockheed Information Systems
3251 Hanover Street
Palo Alto, CA 94304
Telephone (415) 493-4411

SECTION IV
CONGRESSIONAL OFFICES

Congressional Budget Office

2nd and D Streets SW
Washington, DC 20515
Information (202) 225-1491   Public Affairs (202) 225-4416

INFORMATION SOURCES AND SYSTEMS

CONGRESSIONAL SCOREKEEPING SYSTEM

Description: The Congressional Budget Office issues periodic reports on the status of congressional budget action.

The CBO has a series of publications available through GPO on the budget including 5 year budget projections, economic reports and projections, general government programs, human resources, international affairs, national security, and natural resources.

Contact: CBO
Budget Analysis Division
2nd and D Street SW
Washington, DC 20515
Telephone (202) 225-3811

General Accounting Office

441 G Street NW
Washington, DC 20548
Information (202) 275-6202   Reports and Publications (202) 275-6241

INFORMATION SOURCES AND SYSTEMS

LEGISLATIVE AUTHORIZATION PROGRAM INFORMATION SYSTEM

Description: Federal agencies input includes budgetary, program and legislative information. Reports are made in response to committee or member requests.

Contact: GAO
Program Analysis Division
441 G Street NW
Washington, DC 20548
Telephone (202) 275-1811

Government Printing Office

Washington, DC 20042
Inquiry Desk (202) 783-3238

GPO is part of the legislative branch of the U.S. Government. The Superintendent of Documents is the sales arm of GPO. It sells only what GPO prints and that runs to about 20,000 current titles.

PUBLICATIONS

Information Announcements, Selected U.S. Government Publications

Description: These subject bibliographies come out 11 times per year. Subject bibliographies that are of interest to the energy field are as follows:

Astronomy and Astrophysics
Atomic Energy and Nuclear Power
Congressional Budget Office Publications
Energy Conservations and Resources
Federal Council for Science and Technology Publications
Government Accounting Office Publications
Grants and Awards
NASA Science and Technical Publications
National Bureau of Standards Special Publications
National Bureau of Standards Technical Notes
National Science Foundation Publications
National Standard Reference Data Series
Oil Spills and Ocean Dumping
Patents and Trademarks
Radiation and Radioactivity
Solar Energy

Monthly Catalog of U.S. Government Publications

Description: Each month the library and statutory distribution service of GPO assembles new publication entries to produce the *Monthly*

Catalog of U.S. Government Publications. Entries are arranged by the Superintendent of Documents classification number and contain 4 indexes, author, title, subject, and series report. This publication is sold on a subscription basis and is available in many libraries. December issue contains a cummulative index for the year.

Price Lists: A price list is offered for each subject. Price list #36 is called Government Periodicals and lists all periodicals.

Microfilm Catalog

Description: This catalog is a total sales catalog in microfilm entitled GPO Sales Publication Reference File (PRF). Available in 48x microfiche which may be read on a microfiche reader with reductions ranging from 24x to 48x. It is issued bimonthly and sold on subscription. In addition an update to the PRF is sold on subscription and issued bimonthly in alternate months from the basic PRF. Microfiche catalog is available at GPO bookstores.

ORDERING INFORMATION

Description: Information on prices and availability of publications, orders in Washington DC and orders to be charged to a deposit account may be found by calling (202) 783-3238.

Publications may be picked up and paid for at GPO bookstores in Washington DC or ordered through the mail with an enclosed check or money order. For individuals in the Washington DC area who have an immediate need for a publication, they may be picked up at the Laurel, MD, facility.

Deposit accounts may be established by sending a minimum of $50.00. Telephone orders will be accepted and orders may be charged with a deposit account number.

Contact: Superintendent of Documents
GPO
Washington, DC 20042
Telephone (202) 783-3238

Library of Congress

10 First Street SE
Washington DC 20540
General Information (202) 426-5000
Reference Assistance (202) 426-6500

INFORMATION SOURCES

National Referral Center

Description: A free referral service in the area of science and technology. The referral service uses a subject indexed computerized file called information resources by the center. The center's file which is maintained by professional analysis is used primarily by the center's referral specialists. It also is accessible to readers at the Library of Congress through computer terminals located in reading rooms and to federal agencies through RECON computer network operated by DOE. Sources of information are technical libraries, information and document centers, abstracting and indexing services, professional societies, university research bureaus and institutes, federal and state agencies, industrial labs and testing stations.

Contact: Library of Congress
National Referral Center
Washington, DC 20540
Telephone (202) 426-5676

Science and Technology Division, Reference Section

Description: Reference section has computer terminal access to collection. Publications and reports contain information on marketing, industrial research, technology assessment and government R&D.

Science and Technology Division has abstracting services. The division produces Tracer Bulletins and bibliographies of state of art reports, proceedings and government publications.

Contact: Library of Congress
                Science and Technology Division
                Reference Section
                Washington, DC 20540
                Telephone (202) 426-6500

CONGRESSIONAL RESEARCH SERVICE

Bibliographic Citation File

Description: Maintains current awareness file of information in governmen-
                tal, legislative and international organization publications to
                support the research program of CRS.

                Records available to congressional and legislative branch agen-
                cies having access to the Scorpio Information Retrieval Sys-
                tems. Records are available to public via a number of computer
                terminals located in the Main Reading Room of the Library
                of Congress.

Legislative Information File

Description: Up-to-date on-line computer information file containing ana-
                lytical descriptive and status information about all public gen-
                eral bills and resolutions.

                Available to all having access to Library of Congress Scorpio
                Information Retrieval System including a limited number of
                terminals for use by the public in the Library of Congress Main
                Reading rooms. Printed versions by GPO.

Office of Technology Assessment

INFORMATION SOURCES

OFFICE OF INFORMATION

Description: OTA is the advisory arm of the U.S. Congress whose basic function is to help legislative policy makers anticipate and plan for
technological changes. OTA does studies in six major areas.
These are as follows: Energy, Food, Health Materials, Oceans,
Transportation, National Research and Development Policies
and Priorities. OTA works with the Congressional Budget Office, Congressional Research Service and the General Accounting Office in a Research Notification System to exchange research data.

The office of information provides information on publications available to the public. The publications are also available
through GPO.

Contact: OTA
U.S. Congress
Washington, DC 20510
Telephone (202) 224-8711 (Office of Public Affairs)

Indexes

GENERAL

Accelerators - 12, 24

Acoustics - 43, 53, 55

Aeronautics - 35, 55, 58, 61, 79, 80, 81

Aero Propulsion Lab, Wright Patterson AFB - 57

Aerosols - 7, 8

Aerospace - 25, 50, 57, 61, 79, 80, 81, 82, 83, 96

Aerospace Research Application Center, NASA - 83

AGRICOLA - 33

Agriculture - 33, 61, 91

AIAA Technology Information Service, NASA - 81

Air Force - 57, 58

Air Force Geophysics Lab, Hanscom AFB Technical Library - 57

Air Force Information for Industry Office - 59, 60

Air Force Weapons Lab, Kirtland AFB Technical Library - 57, 58

Air Pollution Technical Information Center, EPA - 75, 82

Air Quality (see also Pollution) - 19, 74, 75

Air Quality Planning and Standards, EPA Office of - 74

Air Transportation Research Information Service (ATRIS) - 71

Alloy Data Center, NBS - 44, 45

Ames Laboratory Library - 6

Animal Physiology - 19, 21

Annapolis, Naval Ship R&D Center - 54, 55

Applied Science and Research Applications (ASRA), Information Resources Center - 85

Argonne National Laboratory CONCEPT - 13

Argonne National Laboratory Library - 6

Argonne National Laboratory, National Energy Software Center - 12

Army - 55, 56, 57

Army Material Development and Readiness Command, Science and Technology Division - 56, 57

Army Mobility Equipment Research and Development Command, Ft. Belvoir Technical Library - 56

Army Research, Development and Planning Information for Industry - 59

Army Research Office - 55

Astronomy - 35, 36, 61, 83, 96

Astrophysics - see Aerospace

Atmospheric Sciences - 35, 50, 61, 83

Atomic Collision Cross Section Information Center, NBS - 45

Atomic Energy - see Nuclear Energy

Atomic Energy Levels Data Information Center, NBS - 45

Atomic Transitions Probabilities and Atomic Line Shapes and Shifts, NBS Data Center - 45, 46

Bartlesville Energy Research Center Library - 5

Battelle-Northwest Library and Information Services - 6

Bendix Corporation—Technical Information Center - 6

Bendix Field Engineering Corporation—Technical Library - 6

Berkeley Particle Data Group, Lawrence Berkeley Laboratory - 15

Bettis Atomic Power Laboratory Library - 7

Bibliographic Citation File, Library of Congress - 99

Bibliographic Data File, NTIS - 34

Bibliographies, Energy - 96

Biological Sciences - 6, 7, 8, 10, 17, 19, 20, 21, 35, 50, 81

Biomedical Computing Technology Information Center, Oak Ridge National Laboratory - 25

Biomedical Sciences - 8, 9, 16, 19, 20, 21, 22, 23, 25, 35, 55, 58, 61, 91, 100

Biomedical Sciences (BIOSI), Oak Ridge Information Center Complex - 20

Bolling Field AFB Documents Section, Office of Scientific Research - 58

Bolling Field AFB Technical Library, Office of Science Research - 58

Brookhaven Energy System Optimization Model - 14

Brookhaven National Laboratory, County Energy Data Base - 14

Brookhaven National Laboratory, Energy Model Data Base - 14

Brookhaven National Laboratory Information Centers (see also individual listings) - 14

Brookhaven National Laboratory Library - 7

BRS - 4

Budget Analysis Division, Congressional Budget Office - 94

Building Technology Information, NBS Center for - 50

Catalog, Microfilm, U.S. Government Publications - 97

Catalog, Monthly, U.S. Government Publications - 96, 97

Chemical Kinetics Data Center, NBS - 46

Chemical Propulsion Information Agency, DOD - 53, 54

Chemical Thermodynamics Data Center, NBS - 47, 48

Chemistry - 5, 6, 7, 8, 9, 10, 11, 12, 29, 31, 35, 43, 46, 47, 53, 54, 57, 58, 61, 67, 82, 91

China Lake Technical Information Center, Naval Weapons - 55

CINDAS Data Base, Purdue University - 49, 50

Classified Information - 62, 63

Coal - 5, 18, 19, 23, 27, 32, 50, 66

Coal Data System, USGS - 66

Computerized Information Systems – see Information Retrieval Systems

Computer Program Abstracts, NASA - 81

Computer Sciences - 5, 8, 12, 35, 58

Computer Software Applications: Energy (Directory of) - 36

CONCEPT, Argonne National Laboratory - 13

Congressional Research Service - 99

Conservation Library - 27, 28

Contracts Information System, DOE Projects Information Systems - 29, 30

Controlled Fusion Atomic Data Center, Oak Ridge National Laboratory - 25

COSMIC, NASA - 83

County Energy Data Base, Brookhaven National Laboratory - 14

CRIB Mineral Resources, USGS - 67

Cryogenic Data Center, NBS - 46

Cryogenics - 46, 54

Crystal Data Center, NBS - 49

Custom Searches (NTI Search) - 35

DARCOM - 59

DARPA - 64

David W. Taylor Naval Ship R&D Center, Annapolis - 54, 55

DDC Announcements of Programs, Products, and Services - 62

DDC Central Registry - 61

DDC Data Banks - 60, 61

DDC Ordering and Registration Information - 62, 63

DDC RDT&E - 9, 11
DDC Referral Services - 61
DDC Technical Abstract Bulletin and Indexes - 62
Defense Documentation Center (DDC) - 60, 61, 62, 63, 64
Defense Nuclear Agency Technical Library Division - 52
Department of Defense Information Centers (see also individual listings) - 53, 54
Department of Energy Information Centers (see also individual listings) - 29, 30, 31
Devonian Shale - 5
DIALOG, Lockheed - 4, 10, 11, 43, 91, 92
Diffusion in Metal Data Center, NBS - 49
Directorate for Scientific Technological and International Affairs - 86
Directory of Computerized Data Files, NTIS - 35
Directory of Computer Software Applications: Energy (NTIS) - 36
District Offices, DOC, Predicasts Data Base - 43
Document Delivery Service - 72
Documents Section, Bolling Field AFB, Office of Scientific Research - 58
DOD RDT&E On-Line System - 61
DOD Reports, Unclassified/Unlimited - 63, 64
DOE Energy Data Base, DOE RECON - 18
DOE RECON (see also individual data bases) - 4, 6, 9, 10, 11, 18, 19, 23, 98
DOT Trisnet - 70
Dow Jones Information Systems - 4
Ecological Sciences Information Center, Oak Ridge Information Center Complex - 21, 22
Ecology - see Environmental Sciences
Ecology Information Center, Oak Ridge National Laboratory - 17
Economics - 14, 19, 22, 31, 35, 72, 82, 86, 91, 94
Eco Systems Analysis Data Center, Oak Ridge National Laboratory - 26
Education Resources Information Center - 82
Electric Power - 13, 18, 21, 22, 27, 29, 56

Electrolyte Data Center, NBS - 46
Electronics - 6, 7, 8, 11, 12, 29, 35, 53, 54, 55, 56, 57, 61, 91
Emissions Data Systems, EPA National - 74
ENDEX - 50, 51
Energy and Environmental Response Center, Oak Ridge Information Center Complex - 23
Energy and Environmental Sciences, Oak Ridge Information Center Complex - 21
Energy and Mineral Resources Research Institute, Iowa State University - 31
Energy Conservation - 14, 18, 19, 22, 27, 28, 31, 36, 96
Energy Cost Analysis Program (NECAP), NASA - 83
Energy Data Base EISO, DOE RECON Data Base - 18
Energy Data System, EPA - 75
Energy Information Administration - 31
Energy Model Data Base, Brookhaven National Laboratory - 14
Energy Modeling - 14, 75
Energy Policy - 14, 18, 19, 28, 35, 86
Energy Publications, NTIS - 35, 36, 37, 38
Energy R&D Projects, DOE RECON Data Base - 18
Energy Research and Development Inventory, Oak Ridge Information Center Complex - 22, 23
Energy Safety (nonnuclear) - 26, 27, 30
Energy Supplies and Resources - 14, 19, 22, 31, 35, 37, 51, 75, 79, 80, 81, 86, 96
Engineering - 5, 6, 7, 8, 9, 11, 12, 35, 39, 43, 50, 55, 61, 82, 91
Engineering Index, DOE RECON Data Base - 18
Engineering Sciences Data Unit, London - 39
Environmental Assessment, NOAA Center for - 51
Environmental Data and Information Service, NOAA - 50
Environmental Measurements Laboratory Library - 7
Environmental Microthesaurus—a Hierarchical List of Indexing Terms Used by NTIS - 37
Environmental Monitoring and Support Laboratory, EPA - 75

Environmental Mutagen Information Center, Oak Ridge Information Center Complex - 21

Environmental Response Center, Oak Ridge Information Center Complex - 23

Environmental Sciences - 5, 6, 7, 9, 10, 11, 14, 16, 17, 18, 19, 20, 21, 22, 23, 24, 25, 27, 28, 35, 50, 51, 55, 57, 72, 75, 85, 86, 91

Environmental Teratology Information Center, Oak Ridge Information Center Complex - 21

Federal Council for Science and Technology - 96

Federal Preparedness Agency - 78

Fission - see Nuclear Energy

Fluid Mechanics - 12, 58

Foreign Technology and Translations - 38, 39, 40

Fort Belvoir Technical Library, Army Mobility Equipment Research and Development Command - 56

Fossil Fuel Energy - 5, 13, 19, 21, 22, 23, 31, 32, 35, 36

Franklin Institute Research Laboratory, National Solar Heating and Cooling Solar Documentation Center - 65

Fusion - see Thermonuclear Power

GE CRIB - 67

GE Mark III Worldwide Sharing Network - 66

General Atomic Company Library - 7

General Electric Company—Philadelphia Library - 7

General Electric Company—St. Petersburg Library - 8

Geoecology Data Base, Oak Ridge National Laboratory - 26

Geological Survey, U.S. - 66, 67, 68, 69

Geology - 5, 9, 42, 49, 50, 51, 57, 66, 67

Geophysical and Solar Terrestrial Data Center, NOAA National - 51

Geothermal Energy - see Thermal Energy

Geotherm, USGS - 66

GE R&D Center Data Base - 7

Goddard Space Flight Center, NASA - 83

Goodyear Atomic Corporation Library - 8

Government Periodicals (price list) - 97

Government Reports Announcements and Index, NTIS - 34, 82

Grank Forks Energy Research Center Library - 5

Hanford - 6, 17

Hanscom AFB, Air Force Geophysics Lab Technical Library - 57

Harry Diamond Labs, Science and Technical Information Office - 56

Health - see Medicine, Biomedical Sciences, Industrial Hygiene

Health and Environmental Studies Program, Oak Ridge Information Center Complex - 20

Health and Safety Engineering - 9, 18

Helium Division, Natural Gas Data Base, USGS - 68

High Pressure Data Center - 48

Highway Research Information Services (HRIS) - 71

Highway Safety Literature Service (HSL) - 71

Hydroelectric Power - 13, 31, 50

Hydrology - 13, 18

Idaho National Engineering Laboratory Technical Library - 8

Independent R&D Data Bank - 60

Indiana University/Purdue University, NASA Aerospace Research Application Center - 83

Industrial Hygiene - 10, 21

Industrial Safety (see also Health and Safety Engineering) - 8, 9

Information Announcements, Selected U.S. Government Publications - 96

Information Center Complex, Oak Ridge - 19

Information Center for Energy Safety, Oak Ridge National Laboratory - 26, 27

Information Resources, Library of Congress - 98

Infrared Information and Analysis Center, DOD - 54

Inhalation Toxicology Research Institute Library - 8

Instrumentation - 7, 8, 35

Ion Energetics Data Center, NBS - 47

Iowa State University, Energy and Mineral Resources Research Institute - 31

Isotope Separation - 12

JURIS - 4
Kirtland AFB Technical Library, Air Force Weapons Lab - 57, 58
Kirtland AFB, Weapons Evaluation Facility - 55
Knolls Atomic Power Laboratory Library - 8
Knowledge Availability Systems Center, NASA - 82
Laramie Energy Research Center Library - 5
Lawrence Berkeley Laboratory - 15
Lawrence Berkeley Laboratory Library - 9
Lawrence Livermore Laboratory - 16
Lawrence Livermore Laboratory Library - 9
Legislative Authorization Program Information System - 95
Legislative Information File - 99
Library Network (NALNET), NASA - 79
LMFBR Fuel Cladding Information Center - 17
Lockheed Information Systems - 4, 10, 11, 43, 91, 92
Los Alamos Scientific Laboratory Library - 9
Magnetohydrodynamics - 18
MARC - 4
Maritime Research Information Service (MRIS) - 71
Mason & Hanger, Silas Mason Co., Inc.—Amarillo Library - 9
Materials Science - 6, 7, 8, 9, 26, 35, 48, 49, 53, 58, 68, 91
Mathematics - 5, 6, 7, 8, 9, 10, 11, 12, 36, 43, 55, 58, 61, 91
Mechanical Properties Data Center, Oak Ridge National Laboratory - 25, 26
Mechanics - 43, 53, 54, 55, 58, 83
Medicine - 7, 10, 21, 25, 81, 82, 91, 100
MEDLINE - 4
MERADCOM - 56
Metallurgy - 6, 7, 8, 10, 11, 12, 25, 31, 44, 48, 49, 54, 67, 82, 83
Mid-American Solar Energy Complex - 28
Mineral and Material R&D, USGS Information Systems - 67, 68

Mineral Resources, USGS CRIB - 67
Mining Research, USGS - 68
Molecular Spectra Data Center, NBS - 49
Monthly Catalog of U.S. Government Publications - 96, 97
Morgantown Energy Research Center Library - 5
Mound Facilities Library - 10
NALNET Library Network, NASA - 79
NASA Information Centers - 81, 82, 83
NASA RECON - 4, 80
NASA/SCAN - 80
NASA Science and Technical Publications - 96
National Agricultural Library - 33
National Bureau of Science Information Centers (see also individual listings) - 44, 45, 46, 47, 48, 49, 50
National Bureau of Standards (NBS) - 43, 44, 45, 46, 47, 48, 49, 50, 96
National Bureau of Standards Library - 43
National Bureau of Standards Publications - 96
National Center for Analysis of Energy Systems, Brookhaven National Laboratory - 14
National Center for Thermodynamic Data of Minerals, USGS - 67
National Emissions Data System, EPA - 74
National Energy Information Center - 31
National Energy Software Center, Argonne National Laboratory - 12
National Geothermal Information Resource, Lawrence Berkeley Laboratory - 15
National Nuclear Data Center, Brookhaven National Laboratory - 14
National Oceanic Atmospheric Administration (NOAA) - 50, 51
National Oceanic Atmospheric Administration (NOAA) Information Centers (see also individual listings) - 50, 51
National Referral Center, Library of Congress - 98
National Science Foundation Publications - 96
National Solar Heating and Cooling Information Center - 65
Mineral and Materials Supply/Demand Analysis System, USGS - 68

National Solar Heating and Cooling Solar Documentation Center - 65
National Space Science Data Center - 83
National Standard Reference Data Series - 96
National Standard Reference Data System (NSRDS), NBS - 44
National Technical Information Service (see also NTIS) - 34, 35, 36, 37, 38, 39, 40, 41, 62, 63, 80, 84
National Uranium Resource Evaluation Project, Oak Ridge National Laboratory - 22
Natural Gas - 5, 32, 50, 66, 68
Naval Nuclear Engineering - 8
Naval Research Laboratory, Technical Information Division - 54
Naval Ship R&D Center, Annapolis - 54, 55
Naval Weapons China Lake Technical Information Center - 55
Navy - 54, 55
Navy Acquisition Research and Development Center (NARDIC) - 58, 59
NECAP, NASA - 83
Neutron Data Bibliography, Computerized Index to - 14
Neutron Data File, Computerized Index to - 14
Nevada Operations Office, Nevada Applied Ecology Information Center - 17
New England Research Application Center, NASA - 82
New York Times Information System - 4, 10
NOAA Environmental Data Index (ENDEX) - 50, 51
Nondestructive Testing Information Analysis Center, DOD - 53
North Carolina Science and Technology Research Center, NASA - 82
Northeast Solar Energy Center - 28
NTIS Bibliographic Data File - 34
NTIS Directory of Computerized Data Files - 35
NTI Search Custom Searches - 35
NTIS Energy Publications - 35, 36, 37, 38
NTIS Government Reports Announcements and Index - 34
NTIS Order Information - 40, 41

NTIS Published Searches - 35
NTIS SRIM - 35
NTIS *Tech Notes* - 35
NTIS *Weekly Government Abstracts* - 34
Nuclear Data Project, Oak Ridge National Laboratory - 23, 24
Nuclear Energy - 7, 11, 13, 16, 19, 21, 22, 24, 29, 36, 37, 50, 96
Nuclear Information and Analysis Center, DOD - 52, 53
Nuclear Medicine - 10, 16, 25
Nuclear Reactor Design and Safety - 12, 17, 18, 19, 24, 27, 37, 38, 48, 57, 88
Nuclear Regulatory Commission Reports and Periodicals - 37, 38
Nuclear Safety Information Center, Oak Ridge National Laboratory - 24
Nuclear Safety Information File, DOE RECON Data Base - 18
Nuclear Science - 6, 8, 9, 10, 12, 14, 15, 16, 18, 23, 25, 30, 35, 43, 45, 47, 48, 52, 54, 55, 56, 61, 82
Nuclear Science Abstracts, DOE RECON Data Base - 18
Nuclear Structure Reference, DOE RECON Data Base - 18
Nuclear Weapons - 11, 24, 52, 55, 56, 57
Numerical Data Analysis and Synthesis, NBS Center for Information and - 49, 50
Oak Ridge Associated Universities Library - 10
Oak Ridge Information Center Complex (see also individual listings) - 19, 20, 21, 22, 23
Oak Ridge National Laboratory (see also individual listings) - 17, 18, 19, 20, 21, 22, 23, 24, 25, 26, 27
Oak Ridge National Laboratory Library - 10, 12
Oak Ridge Technical Information Center - 18
Oceanography - 7, 35, 36, 54, 61, 100
OCLC - 4
OCS Reference Center, USGS - 68, 69
Office of Air Quality Planning and Standards, EPA - 74
Office of Energy Data and Interpretation - 31, 32
Office of Science Research, Bolling Field AFB Technical Library - 58

Office of Scientific Research, Bolling
  Field AFB, Documents Section - 58
Office of Technology Assessment and
  Forecast - 42
Office of Technology Utilization,
  NASA - 81
Oil - see Petroleum
Oil Shale - 5, 18, 23, 27, 31, 32, 67
Oil Shale Data Bank, USGS - 67
Optics - 43, 54
ORBIT, SDC - 4, 10, 11
Ordering and Registration Information,
  DDC - 62, 63
Ordering Information, Government
  Printing Office - 97
Ordering Information, NTIS Publica-
  tions - 40, 41
Ordnance - 11, 35, 56, 61
Orlook System, Oak Ridge National
  Laboratory - 27
Patent Abstracts, NASA - 81
Patent Information - 38, 41, 42, 83,
  84, 96
Patent Search Files - 41
Periodic Bibliographies, NASA - 81
Petroleum - 5, 18, 27, 31, 32, 36, 37,
  39, 66, 68
Petroleum Data Systems, USGS - 66
Photonuclear Data Center, NBS - 47
Physical Sciences - 5, 9, 10, 12, 43,
  82, 91
Physics - 5, 6, 7, 8, 9, 10, 11, 12, 43,
  50, 51, 53, 57, 58, 61, 83, 91
Pittsburgh Energy Research Center
  Library - 5
Plasma Physics - 10, 45
Plastics - 6
Policy Research and Analysis, Division
  of - 86
Pollution - 16, 19, 20, 23, 35, 75, 82,
  88, 96
Potential Defense Contractors Program -
  64
Power Information Center, DOD/
  NASA/NSF/DOE - 29
Predicasts Data Base, Lockheed
  DIALOG - 43
Princeton University, Plasma Physics
  Laboratory, Library - 10
Program Analysis Division, General
  Accounting Office - 95
Propellants and Missiles - 56, 57, 61, 81

Publications, Government - see Govern-
  ment Printing Office chapter
Published Searches, NTIS - 35
Purdue University, CINDAS Data Base -
  49, 50
Radiation Chemistry Data Center,
  NBS/DOE - 30
Radiation Doses and Safety - 10, 17, 24,
  52, 54, 56, 57, 88, 96
Radiation Laboratory, University of
  Notre Dame - 30
Radiation Shielding Information Center,
  Oak Ridge National Laboratory - 24,
  25
Radioactive Decay - 14, 30, 96
Radiological Sciences (see also Nuclear
  Science) - 6, 7, 30, 56, 88, 96
Radionuclides - 16, 17, 18, 24, 30
Railroad Research Information Service
  (RRIS) - 71
R&DPP - 60
R&D Reports, Department of Energy - 7
R&T Work Unit Information System -
  60
Rare Earth Information Center, DOE - 31
RECON, DOE - 4, 6, 9, 10, 11, 18, 19,
  23, 98
RECON, NASA - 4, 80
Redstone Scientific Information Center -
  56
Reports on Energy Information Re-
  ported to Congress, NTIS - 37
Research and Technology Objectives and
  Plans Summary, NASA - 79
Research Materials Information Center,
  Oak Ridge National Laboratory - 26
Research Projects Information Systems,
  DOE Project Information Systems - 30
Research Triangle Park, Army Research
  Office - 55
Research Triangle Park, EPA Offices -
  74, 75
Research Triangle Park, NASA, North
  Carolina Science and Technology Re-
  search Center - 82
RESPONSA - 18
Reynolds Electrical and Engineering Co.
  Technical Library - 10
Rockwell International Library - 11
Sandia Laboratories Library, Albuquer-
  que - 11

Sandia Laboratories Library, Livermore - 11

Savannah River Laboratory Library - 11

SCAN, NASA - 80

Science and Technical Publications, NASA - 96

Science and Technology Division, Army Material Development and Readiness Command - 56, 57

Science and Technology Division, Reference Section, Library of Congress - 98, 99

Science and Technology, Federal Council for - 96

Science and Technology Information Office, NASA - 79, 80, 81

Science Resources Studies, NSF - 86, 87

Scientific and Technical Aerospace Reports, NASA (STAR) - 80

Scientific and Technical Information System, NASA - 80

Scientific Library at the Patent and Trademark Office - 41

Scientific Technological and International Affairs, Directorate for - 86

Scorpio, Library of Congress - 99

SDC ORBIT - 4, 10, 11, 91

Search Services, Smithsonian Science Information Exchange - 90, 91

Solar Energy - 7, 18, 19, 27, 28, 29, 36, 37, 42, 50, 65, 80, 96

Solar Energy Research Institute - 28, 29

Solid Fuels - 5

Solid State Physics - 11, 26, 31, 54, 58

Solid Waste Information Retrieval System, EPA - 75

Southwest Research Institute Library - 11

Space - see Aerospace

Space Power Systems - 11

Space Science Data Center, National - 83

Spectroscopy - 5, 16, 30, 46, 44, 45, 47, 48, 49, 53, 54, 56

Solar Heating and Cooling, National Information Center - 65

Solar Heating and Cooling, National Solar Documentation Center - 65

Southern Energy/Environmental Information Center - 27

SRIM, NTIS - 35

SSIE—On-Line Search Services - 91, 92

Standard Reference Data Series, National - 96

Stanford Linear Accelerator Library - 12

Superconductive Materials Data Center, NBS - 48

Superintendent of Documents - 80

Table of Isotopes Project, Lawrence Berkeley Laboratory - 15

Tar Sands - 5

Technical Abstract Bulletin and Indexes, DDC - 62

Technical Information Center at Oak Ridge - 18

Technical Information Services, AIAA - 81

Technical Report Data Bank - 60

Technology Application Center, NASA - 82

Technology Utilization Branch, NASA - 81

Tech Notes, NTIS - 35

Thermal Energy - 7, 13, 15, 18, 19, 27, 36, 66

Thermodynamic Data of Minerals, USGS National Center for - 67

Thermodynamics - 46, 47, 53, 54, 56, 67, 83

Thermodynamics Research Center, NBS - 47

Thermonuclear Power - 10, 18, 25, 27, 36

Thermophysical and Electric Properties Information Analysis Center, DOD/CINDAS - 53

Thorium - 22

Toxic Materials Data Base, DOE RECON - 18

Toxic Materials Information Center, Oak Ridge Information Center Complex - 23

Toxicology - 19, 20, 21, 23

Toxicology Data Bank, Oak Ridge Information Center Complex - 20

Toxicology Information Response Center, Oak Ridge Information Center Complex - 21

TRANSDEX Index - 40

Transit Research Information Center (TRIC) - 71

Transportation Research Board - 71

Tri Service Industry Information Center - 58, 59, 60
Trisnet, DOT - 70
Tris On-Line Service - 72
Unclassified Publications - 9, 12, 38, 63, 64
Unclassified/Unlimited DOD Reports - 63, 64
Union Carbide Corporation K-25 Plant Library - 12
Union Carbide Corporation Y-12 Plant Library - 12
Union Carbide Nuclear Division, Oak Ridge National Laboratory - 27
University of New Mexico, NASA Technology Application Center - 82
University of Notre Dame, Radiation Laboratory - 30
University of Oklahoma CRIB - 67
University of Pittsburgh, NASA Knowledge Availability Systems Center - 82
University of Southern California, Western Research Application Center, NASA - 82
Uranium - 6, 8, 22
Urban Mass Transit Administration - 71

U.S. Bureau of Mines - 68
U.S. Geological Survey (USGS) (see also individual listings) - 66, 67, 68, 69
USGS Systems (see also individual listings) - 66, 67, 68
U.S. Resources, Data Bank on - 78
Water Quality (see also Pollution) - 19
Water Resources Abstracts, DOE RECON Data Base - 18
Weapons Evaluation Facility, Albuquerque (Kirtland AFB) - 55
Weekly Government Abstracts, NTIS - 34
Well History Control Systems, USGS - 66
Western Regional Solar Energy Center - 28
Western Research Application Center, NASA - 82
Westinghouse Hanford - 6, 17
Wind Power - 7, 42, 80
Worldwide Inventory, Information Services on Research in Progress - 39
Wright Patterson AFB, Aero Propulsion Lab - 57
X-ray and Ionizing Radiation Data Center, NBS - 48

INFORMATION CENTERS

Aero Propulsion Lab, Wright Patterson AFB - 57
Aerospace Research Application Center, NASA - 83
Air Force Information for Industry Office - 59, 60
Air Pollution Technical Information Center, EPA - 75, 82
Air Quality Planning and Standards, EPA Office of - 74
Air Transportation Research Information Service (ATRIS) - 71
Alloy Data Center, NBS - 44, 45
Annapolis, Naval Ship R&D Center - 54, 55
Applied Science and Research Applications (ASRA), Information Resources Center - 85

Argonne National Laboratory, National Energy Software Center - 12
Army Material Development and Readiness Command, Science and Technology Division - 56, 57
Army Research, Development and Planning Information for Industry - 59
Army Research Office - 55
Atomic Collision Cross Section Information Center, NBS - 45
Atomic Energy Levels Data Information Center, NBS - 45
Atomic Transitions Probabilities and Atomic Line Shapes and Shifts, NBS Data Center - 45, 46
Berkeley Particle Data Group, Lawrence Berkeley Laboratory - 15

Biomedical Computing Technology Information Center, Oak Ridge National Laboratory - 25

Biomedical Sciences (BIOSI), Oak Ridge Information Center Complex - 20

Bolling Field AFB Documents Section, Office of Scientific Research - 58

Brookhaven National Laboratory Information Centers (see also individual listings) - 14

Building Technology Information, NBS Center for - 50

Chemical Kinetics Data Center, NBS - 46

Chemical Propulsion Information Agency, DOD - 53, 54

Chemical Thermodynamics Data Center, NBS - 47, 48

China Lake Technical Information Center, Naval Weapons - 55

Contracts Information System, DOE Project Information Systems - 29, 30

Controlled Fusion Atomic Data Center, Oak Ridge National Laboratory - 25

Cryogenic Data Center, NBS - 46

Crystal Data Center, NBS - 49

David W. Taylor Naval Ship R&D Center, Annapolis - 54, 55

Defense Documentation Center - 60, 61, 62, 63, 64

Department of Defense Information Centers (see also individual listings) - 53, 54

Department of Energy Information Centers (see also individual listings) - 29, 30, 31

Diffusion in Metal Data Center, NBS - 49

Documents Section, Bolling Field AFB, Office of Scientific Research - 58

Ecological Sciences Information Center, Oak Ridge Information Center Complex - 21, 22

Ecology Information Center, Oak Ridge National Laboratory - 17

Eco Systems Analysis Data Center, Oak Ridge National Laboratory - 26

Education Resources Information Center - 82

Electrolyte Data Center, NBS - 46

Energy and Environmental Response Center, Oak Ridge Information Center Complex - 23

Energy and Environmental Sciences, Oak Ridge Information Center Complex - 21

Energy and Mineral Resources Research Institute, Iowa State University - 31

Energy Research and Development Inventory, Oak Ridge Information Center Complex - 22, 23

Environmental Assessment, NOAA Center for - 51

Environmental Data and Information Service, NOAA - 50

Environmental Monitoring and Support Laboratory, EPA - 75

Environmental Mutagen Information Center, Oak Ridge Information Center Complex - 21

Environmental Response Center, Oak Ridge Information Center Complex - 23

Environmental Teratology Information Center, Oak Ridge Information Center Complex - 21

Franklin Institute Research Laboratory, National Solar Heating and Cooling Solar Documentation Center - 65

Geophysical and Solar Terrestrial Data Center, NOAA National - 51

Goddard Space Flight Center, NASA - 83

Hanford - 6, 17

Harry Diamond Labs, Science and Technical Information Office - 56

Health and Environmental Studies Program, Oak Ridge Information Center Complex - 20

High Pressure Data Center - 48

Highway Research Information Services (HRIS) - 71

Highway Safety Literature Service (HSL) - 71

Indiana University/Purdue University, NASA Aerospace Research Application Center - 83

Information Center Complex, Oak Ridge - 19

Information Center for Energy Safety, Oak Ridge National Laboratory - 26, 27

Infrared Information and Analysis Center, DOD - 54

Ion Energetics Data Center, NBS - 47

Iowa State University, Energy and Mineral Resources Research Institute - 31

Kirtland AFB, Weapons Evaluation Facility - 55
Knowledge Availability Systems Center, NASA - 82
Lawrence Berkeley Laboratory - 15
Lawrence Livermore Laboratory - 16
LMFBR Fuel Cladding Information Center - 17
Maritime Research Information Service (MRIS) - 71
Mechanical Properties Data Center, Oak Ridge National Laboratory - 25, 26
Mid-American Solar Energy Complex - 28
Mineral and Material R&D, USGS Information Systems - 67, 68
Mining Research, USGS - 68
Molecular Spectra Data Center, NBS - 49
NASA Information Centers - 81, 82, 83
National Bureau of Science Information Centers (see also individual listings) - 44, 45, 46, 47, 48, 49, 50
National Center for Analysis of Energy Systems, Brookhaven National Laboratory - 14
National Center for Thermodynamic Data of Minerals, USGS - 67
National Energy Information Center - 31
National Energy Software Center, Argonne National Laboratory - 12
National Geothermal Information Resource, Lawrence Berkeley Laboratory - 15
National Nuclear Data Center, Brookhaven National Laboratory - 14
National Oceanic Atmospheric Administration (NOAA) Information Centers (see also individual listings) - 50, 51
National Solar Heating and Cooling Information Center - 65
National Solar Heating and Cooling Solar Documentation Center - 65
National Space Science Data Center - 83
National Standard Reference Data System (NSRDS), NBS - 44
National Uranium Resource Evaluation Project, Oak Ridge National Laboratory - 22

Naval Research Laboratory, Technical Information Division - 54
Naval Ship R&D Center, Annapolis - 54, 55
Naval Weapons China Lake Technical Information Center - 55
Navy Acquisition Research and Development Center (NARDIC) - 58, 59
Nevada Operations Office, Nevada Applied Ecology Information Center - 17
New England Research Application Center, NASA - 82
Nondestructive Testing Information Analysis Center, DOD - 53
North Carolina Science and Technology Research Center, NASA - 82
Northeast Solar Energy Center - 28
Nuclear Data Project, Oak Ridge National Laboratory - 23, 24
Nuclear Information and Analysis Center, DOD - 52, 53
Nuclear Safety Information Center, Oak Ridge National Laboratory - 24
Numerical Data Analysis and Synthesis, NBS Center for Information and - 49, 50
Oak Ridge Information Center Complex (see also individual listings) - 19, 20, 21, 22, 23
Oak Ridge National Laboratory (see also individual listings) - 17, 18, 19, 20, 21, 22, 23, 24, 25, 26, 27
Oak Ridge Technical Information Center - 18
OCS Reference Center, USGS - 68, 69
Office of Air Quality Planning and Standards, EPA - 74
Office of Energy Data and Interpretation - 31, 32
Office of Scientific Research, Bolling Field AFB, Documents Section - 58
Office of Technology Utilization, NASA - 81
Orlook System, Oak Ridge National Laboratory - 27
Photonuclear Data Center, NBS - 47
Power Information Center, DOD/NASA/NSF/DOE - 29
Radiation Chemistry Data Center, NBS/DOE - 30
Radiation Laboratory, University of Notre Dame - 30

Radiation Shielding Information Center, Oak Ridge National Laboratory - 24, 25

Railroad Research Information Service (RRIS) - 71

Rare Earth Information Center, DOE - 31

Redstone Scientific Information Center - 56

Research Materials Information Center, Oak Ridge National Laboratory - 26

Research Projects Information Systems, DOE Project Information Systems - 30

Research Triangle Park, Army Research Office - 55

Research Triangle Park, EPA Offices - 74, 75

Research Triangle Park, NASA, North Carolina Science and Technology Research Center - 82

Science and Technology Division, Army Material Development and Readiness Command - 56, 57

Science and Technology Information Office, NASA - 79, 80, 81

Solar Energy Research Institute - 28, 29

Solar Heating and Cooling, National Information Center - 65

Solar Heating and Cooling, National Solar Documentation Center - 65

Southern Energy/Environmental Information Center - 27

Space Science Data Center, National - 83

Superconductive Materials Data Center, NBS - 48

Table of Isotopes Project, Lawrence Berkeley Laboratory - 15

Technical Information Center at Oak Ridge - 18

Technical Information Services, AIAA - 81

Technology Application Center, NASA - 82

Technology Utilization Branch, NASA - 81

Thermodynamic Data of Minerals, USGS National Center for - 67

Thermodynamics Research Center, NBS - 47

Thermophysical and Electric Properties Information Analysis Center, DOD/CINDAS - 53

Toxic Materials Information Center, Oak Ridge Information Center Complex - 23

Toxicology Data Bank, Oak Ridge Information Center Complex - 20

Toxicology Information Response Center, Oak Ridge Information Center Complex - 21

Transit Research Information Center (TRIC) - 71

Tri Service Industry Information Center - 58, 59, 60

Trisnet, DOT - 70

Union Carbide Nuclear Division, Oak Ridge National Laboratory - 27

University of New Mexico, NASA Technology Application Center - 82

University of Notre Dame, Radiation Laboratory - 30

University of Pittsburgh, NASA Knowledge Availability Systems Center - 82

University of Southern California, Western Research Application Center, NASA - 82

U.S. Geological Survey (see also individual listings) - 66, 67, 68

Weapons Evaluation Facility, Albuquerque (Kirtland AFB) - 55

Western Regional Solar Energy Center - 28

Western Research Application Center, NASA - 82

Westinghouse Hanford - 6, 17

Wright Patterson AFB, Aero Propulsion Lab - 57

X-ray and Ionizing Radiation Data Center, NBS - 48

INFORMATION RETRIEVAL SYSTEMS

AGRICOLA - 33
AIAA Technology Information Service, NASA - 81
Argonne National Laboratory CONCEPT - 13
Bibliographic Citation File, Library of Congress - 99
Bibliographic Data File, NTIS - 34
Brookhaven Energy System Optimization Model - 14
Brookhaven National Laboratory, County Energy Data Base - 14
Brookhaven National Laboratory, Energy Model Data Base - 14
BRS - 4
CINDAS Data Base, Purdue University - 49, 50
Coal Data System, USGS - 66
CONCEPT, Argonne National Laboratory - 13
COSMIC, NASA - 83
County Energy Data Base, Brookhaven National Laboratory - 14
CRIB Mineral Resources, USGS - 67
Custom Searches (NTISearch) - 35
DDC Data Banks - 60, 61
DDC RDT&E - 9, 11
DDC Referral Service - 61
DIALOG Lockheed - 4, 10, 11, 43, 91, 92
District Offices, DOC, Predicasts Data Base - 43
DOD RDT&E On-Line System - 61
DOE Energy Data Base, DOE RECON - 18
DOE RECON (see also individual data bases) - 4, 6, 9, 10, 11, 18, 19, 23, 98
DOT Trisnet - 70
Dow Jones Information System - 4
Emissions Data Systems, EPA National - 74
ENDEX - 50, 51
Energy Cost Analysis Program (NECAP), NASA - 83
Energy Data Base EISO, DOE RECON Data Base - 18
Energy Data System, EPA - 75
Energy Model Data Base, Brookhaven National Laboratory - 14

Energy R&D Projects, DOE RECON Data Base - 18
Engineering Index, DOE RECON Data Base - 18
Engineering Sciences Data Unit, London - 39
GE CRIB - 67
GE Mark III Worldwide Sharing Network - 66
Geoecology Data Base, Oak Ridge National Laboratory - 26
Geotherm, USGS - 66
GE R&D Center Data Base - 7
Helium Division Natural Gas Data Base, USGS - 68
Independent R&D Data Bank - 60
Information Resources, Library of Congress - 98
JURIS - 4
Legislative Information File - 99
Library Network (NALNET), NASA - 79
Lockheed Information System - 4, 10, 11, 43, 91, 92
MEDLINE - 4
Mineral and Materials Supply/Demand Analysis System, USGS - 68
Mineral Resources, USGS CRIB - 67
NALNET Library Network, NASA - 79
National Emissions Data System, EPA - 74
NASA RECON - 4, 80
NASA/SCAN - 80
National Referral Center, Library of Congress - 98
NECAP, NASA - 83
Neutron Data Bibliography, Computerized Index to - 14
Neutron Data File, Computerized Index to - 14
New York Times Information System - 4, 10
NOAA Environmental Data Index (ENDEX) - 50, 51
NTIS Bibliographic Data File - 34
NTISearch Custom Searches - 35
NTIS SRIM - 35
Nuclear Safety Information File, DOE RECON Data Base - 18

Nuclear Science Abstracts, DOE
  RECON Data Base - 18
Nuclear Structure Reference, DOE
  RECON Data Base - 18
OCLC - 4
Oil Shale Data Bank, USGS - 67
ORBIT, SDC - 4, 10, 11
Petroleum Data Systems, USGS - 66
Predicasts Data Base, Lockheed
  DIALOG - 43
Purdue University, CINDAS Data
  Base - 49, 50
R&DPP - 60
R&T Work Unit Information System -
  60
RECON, DOE - 4, 6, 9, 10, 11, 18, 19,
  23, 98
RECON, NASA - 4, 80
RESPONSA - 18
SCAN, NASA - 80
Science and Technology Division, Ref-
  erence Section, Library of Congress -
  98, 99

Scientific and Technical Information
  System, NASA - 80
Scorpio, Library of Congress - 99
SDC ORBIT - 4, 10, 11, 91
Search Services, Smithsonian Science
  Information Exchange - 90, 91
Solid Waste Information Retrieval
  System, EPA - 75
SRIM, NTIS - 35
SSIE On-Line Search Service - 91, 92
Technical Report Data Bank - 60
Toxic Materials Data Base, DOE
  RECON - 18
TRANSDEX Index - 40
Tris On-Line Service - 72
University of Oklahoma CRIB - 67
USGS Systems (see also individual
  listings) - 66, 67, 68
U.S. Resources, Data Bank on – 78
Water Resources Abstracts, DOE
  RECON Data Base - 18
Well History Control System, USGS -
  66

LIBRARIES

Albuquerque, Sandia Laboratories - 11
Amarillo—Mason & Hanger, Silas
  Mason Co., Inc. - 9
Ames Laboratory - 6
Argonne National Laboratory - 6
Bartlesville Energy Research Center - 5
Bendix Corporation—Technical Infor-
  mation Center - 6
Bendix Field Engineering Corporation,
  Technical - 6
Berkeley, California ITS/LIB - 72
Bettis Atomic Power Laboratory - 7
Bolling Field AFB Office of Science
  Research - 58
Bonneville Power Administration, In-
  formation Center and Library - 13
Brookhaven National Laboratory - 7
Conservation - 27, 28
Defense Nuclear Agency Technical,
  Library Division - 52
Department of Energy - 4
Department of Transportation - 70

DOT/LIB - 72
Environmental Measurements Labora-
  tory - 7
Environmental Protection Agency - 74
Fort Belvoir Technical, Army Mobility
  Equipment Research and Development
  Command - 56
General Atomic Company - 7
General Electric, Philadelphia - 7
General Electric, St. Petersburg - 8
Georgia Tech - 27
Goodyear Atomic Corporation - 8
Grand Forks Energy Research Center - 5
Hanscom AFB Geophysics Lab, Tech-
  nical - 57
Idaho National Engineering Laboratory,
  Technical - 8
Information Services, Battelle—North-
  west Library and - 6
Inhalation Toxicology Research In-
  stitute - 8
ITS/LIB - 72

Kirtland AFB Weapons Lab, Technical - 57, 58
Knolls Atomic Power Laboratory - 8
Laramie Energy Research Center - 5
Lawrence Berkeley Laboratory - 9
Lawrence Livermore Laboratory - 9
Los Alamos Scientific Laboratory - 9
Morgantown Energy Research Center - 5
Mound Facilities - 10
National Agricultural - 33
National Bureau of Standards - 43
Northwestern University Transportation Center Library - 72
Nuclear Regulatory Commission - 88
Oak Ridge Associated Universities - 10
Oak Ridge National Laboratory - 10, 12
Pittsburgh Energy Research Center - 5

Reynolds Electrical and Engineering Co., Technical - 10
Rockwell International - 11
Sandia Laboratories, Livermore - 11
Savannah River Laboratory - 11
Scientific, at the Patent and Trademark Office - 41
Southwest Research Institute - 11
Stanford Linear Accelerator - 12
Technical Documentation Center, DOT - 72
Technical Information Center, DOT - 72
Transportation Center Library, Northwestern University - 72
Union Carbide K-25 Plant - 12
Union Carbide Corporation Y-12 Plant - 12
Princeton University, Plasma Physics Laboratory - 10

ENERGY FROM SOLID WASTE 1979
RECENT DEVELOPMENTS

Edited by Francis A. Domino

Energy Technology Review No. 42
Pollution Technology Review No. 56

The emphasis in the field of solid waste has shifted from disposal to utilization. Vast stores of energy are waiting to be tapped through competent technology.

When we consider that every day each resident of the United States generates about four pounds of waste from products of great diversity, it is apparent that solid waste may someday serve as a sizeable source of energy. But first technical and environmental aspects, as well as social, legal and economic factors, will have to be examined in depth. This book reviews the many phases of waste disposal and energy recovery, discussing recently tested technology. It describes plants presently producing power from refuse while also salvaging material. Technological difficulties are also discussed. It also presents a proposed waste utilization system for the city of New York, as an example that could be applied to other cities.

The final chapter offers greatly detailed recommendations for municipal officials on waste processing and energy recovery plants.

Examples of some important subtitles are found along with chapter headings in the partial, condensed table of contents given below:

1. **OVERVIEW OF ENERGY RECOVERY**
   Preprocessing Techniques
   Incineration
   Pyrolysis
   Biodegradation—Composting, Methane
     Production, Biochemical Processes

2. **NASHVILLE THERMAL TRANSFER
   CORPORATION PLANT**
   Components of Plant—Refuse Handling,
     Grates, Residue Removal
   Major Problems—Emission, Corrosion

3. **ST. LOUIS DEMONSTRATION PLANT**
   Equipment Evaluation
   Characteristics and Costs
   Environmental Evaluations
   Electrostatic Precipitator Performance

4. **COMBUSTION POWER UNIT (CPU-400)
   PILOT PLANT, CALIFORNIA**
   Vertical Combustor & Support Equipment
   Hot Gas System—Particle Collection,
     Residue Removal
   Controls, Instruments, Gas Analysis

5. **COLUMBIA PLAN, NEW YORK, N.Y.**
   Recommendations

Cost Benefit Analyses
Markets for Energy Products
Solid Waste Receiving and Processing
Reclaiming Matter in Metal Recovery
Economics of Purox Gas Utilization

6. **TECHNICAL EVALUATION OF
   PYROLYSIS SYSTEMS**
   Vertical Furnace—Occidental "Flash"
     Pyrolysis
   Rotary Kiln—Monsanto "Landgard"
     Process
   Vertical Shaft Furnace—Union Carbide
     "Purox" Process
   Vertical Shaft Furnace—Hamilton
     Standard "Refu-Cycler" Process

7. **FUEL AND ENERGY FROM WASTE
   BY BIOCONVERSION**
   Major Waste Streams—Agricultural,
     Animal, Forestry, Municipal, Industrial
   Nonproteinaceous Bioconversion of
     Cellulosic Wastes
   Hydrolysis of Cellulose
   Anaerobic Digestion
   Biophotolysis
   Economic Analysis
   Comparison to Other Energy Recovery

8. **ENVIRONMENTAL ASPECTS**
   Federal and State Air Pollution Curbs
   Emissions from Waste-Energy Processes
   Waterwall Incineration
   Refuse-Derived Solid Fuel Processing
   Pyrolysis Gas Processing and Use
   Emission Control and Costs
   Water Pollution Considerations
   Solid Residue Disposal
   Noise and Other Occupational Health Data

9. **MUNICIPAL SCALE THERMAL
   PROCESSING OF SOLID WASTE**
   Incineration and Pyrolysis
   Costs
   Site Layout and Plant Design
   Public Acceptance
   Utilities—Electric, Water, Communication
   Precombustion of Solid Waste
   Incinerator Furnace Design
   Instrumentation
   Control of Liquid and Solid Effluents
   Air Pollution Control
   Special Solid Wastes—Plastics,
     Obnoxious Wastes, Sewage Sludge

ISBN 0-8155-0750-X

321 pages

HEAT PUMP TECHNOLOGY FOR SAVING ENERGY 1979

Edited by M.J. Collie

Energy Technology Review No. 39

With energy costs escalating and fossil fuel supplies diminishing, the heat pump is becoming attractive for residential space heating and cooling because of its high efficiency. This book compares its overall efficiency to that of electrical resistance and fossil fuel heating, covering air-source and water-source pumps, and single-package and split-system units.

It reports on computer-simulated studies of residential heating in 9 cities in which a heat pump replaced a gas or oil furnace, and on tests of heat pumps in buildings in Washington, D.C., Hanover, New Hampshire, and Albuquerque, New Mexico. Data on the Annual Cycle Energy House, in which a heat pump, thermal storage and solar assistance provide space heating, cooling and water heating, attest to energy saved, as do the solar-assisted heat pumps in other areas.

Because early heat pumps had design deficiencies, improvements were mandated. The latter chapters examine modifications such as capacity control to alter refrigerant flow.

Following is a condensed table of contents with **examples of some** important subtitles.

1. HEAT PUMP DESCRIPTION
Air-to-Air Heat Pump
Alternate Configurations
Commercial and Residential Use
Efficiency and Reliability
Thermodynamic Operating Cycle
Design-Related Problems
New Developments

2. WATER- AND AIR-SOURCE PUMPS COMPARED
Commercial Availability
Typical Seasonal Performance
Parametric Results
Heating and Cooling Model

3. RESIDENTIAL AIR-TO-AIR PUMP EVALUATED
Causes of Operating Failure
Influence of Climatic Region
Installation and Maintenance
Market Acceptance
Effect of Air Conditioning on Market
Costs of Competing Systems
Computer-Simulated Energy Use Data
Selection of Test Cities

Effect on Electric Utility Load

4. THREE EXPERIMENTAL STUDIES
Air-to-Air Pump in Washington Home
    Comparison to Fossil-Fueled System
Water-to-Water Pump Using Waste Heat
    in Hanover, New Hampshire
    Economic Benefits
    Energy Savings
System with Thermal Storage in Albuquerque, New Mexico, Office
    Water-to-Water vs Air-to-Air
    Instrumentation and Monitoring

5. ANNUAL CYCLE ENERGY SYSTEM HOUSE
Seasonal Heating and Cooling Loads
Predicted Energy Consumption
Component Specs. and Design Data

6. SOLAR-ASSISTED HEAT PUMP
Phoenix House, Colorado Springs Study
    Heat Loss Analysis
    Storage System Energy Transfer
    Cost Estimates
Saratoga, NY Demonstration Project
    Heating and Cooling Modes
    Major Components
Water-to-Water vs Air-to-Air at SUNY, Albany, NY
    Design Features
    Heating Demand
    Economic Analysis

7. EVALUATING 3-TON HEAT PUMP
Heating Capacity and Coefficient of Performance
Fan Performance—Indoor, Outdoor
Heat Exchanger and Capillary Tube
Performance—Condenser, Evaporator
Compressor Operation
Effect of Variable Refrigerant Charge

8. CAPACITY-CONTROLLED HEAT PUMPS
Comparison to Conventional Systems
Effect of Fan Power
Suction-Valve Cut-off and Design

9. NOISE CONTROL
Proper Placement to Minimize Noise
Enclosure Design
Reducing Compressor/Fan Sound

ISBN 0-8155-0744-5

348 pages